W9-AEJ-872

TABLE OF CONTENTS

FOREWORD

Several years ago at a conference in Birmingham, Alabama, I was in a tailspin. My organization was sponsoring the event and I could tell that it wasn't going well. The first presenter had been aloof—and worse, had no background whatsoever in real-world education. The second had some experience, but almost put us to sleep reading his presentation verbatim. It was now after lunch, a difficult time at best for a presenter. Dr. Steven Edwards was scheduled for that afternoon. He had been a successful principal, had an easy confidence about him, and seemed eager to get started. That was good. I watched the audience as Steve began to unfold his message. He told how he inherited an urban school with falling scores, challenging students, and a flustered faculty. His stories rang true and I watched as heads began to nod in agreement and understanding. Steve shared the obstacles, his fundamentals, and the methods that he used to turn around his school. He touched our hearts as he shared some difficult stories about his students. He lifted our spirits as he counted the successes, one student at a time. He opened our eyes when he shared the simple but essential principles of leadership. Then he paused to allow the participants, seated at roundtables in school district teams, to discuss the ideas he had presented—and that's when the dam broke.

A hubbub of conversation began immediately, and I watched as the discussion rose across the room. Steve moved from table to table assisting where he could, but most were busy talking about pyramids of intervention, pillars of leadership, and ways to use the ideas in their own schools. After a bit, Steve continued with his presentation, interweaving his academic command of leadership with his practical, real-life experience and his engaging, story-telling style. When the day was over, several tables remained and continued their discussions for over an hour! I approached one of the remaining tables and asked the district superintendent what he thought. Known for his straight-forward, no-nonsense talk, the superintendent replied, "After the first two I was about ready to take my team and go home, but Steve Edwards was a home run!"

Paul Chapman met Steve while working on an evaluation of a professional development series for school principals, a series that included Steve as a keynote speaker at the opening event. They immediately connected and engaged one other and series participants in conversations about leadership and how to help people realize their full potential through collaboration and teamwork. Paul's teaching and leadership experience in the public schools, combined with his experience in higher education building and instructing in leadership preparation programs—not to mention his energetic approach to life in general—was a perfect complement to Steve. When these two are discussing how to create dynamic school cultures to enhance overall student achievement and success, their enthusiasm is contagious.

I have now heard Steve present on several occasions. Steve's ideas, stories, and experiences, along with Paul's academic viewpoint, will improve the skills of any leader and the capacity of any faculty. *Six Pillars of Dynamic Schools* will be an excellent book study for central office administrators, district principals, and school faculties that are working on the work of teaching and learning. Steve and Paul's ideas will provide excellent nourishment for professional learning communities to strengthen and nurture the qualities needed for growing successful students. It's a demanding job, but Steve Edwards, Paul Chapman, and *Six Pillars* could be the bright spot that you are seeking—it certainly was for me on a trying day in Birmingham, Alabama.

Dr. John Draper
Chief Executive Officer
Educational Research Service

ABOUT THE AUTHORS

Steven W. Edwards, Ph.D.

A leader nationally recognized by *USA Today* for his innovative approach to education, Dr. Edwards successfully implemented numerous programs to improve student performance during his 16-year tenure as a school administrator. Dr. Edwards has also been instrumental in helping countless school districts tailor similar programs, with positive, far-reaching results. In addition, Dr. Edwards is an internationally recognized keynote speaker, facilitator, and trainer regularly featured as a content expert on television and radio, with appearances on CNN on topics such as school safety, school climate and reform, and strategic planning. Throughout his 30-year professional career, Dr. Edwards has published numerous articles on school reform and leadership, and has co-authored four books that address school reform initiatives and leadership development. He has also served as a professor of educational leadership for both the University of Connecticut and the George Washington University, teaching prospective administrators in the Graduate School of Education. In addition, Dr. Edwards has served as the Vice President for the Children, Communities, and Youth Division of the National Crime Prevention Council in Washington, D.C., where he oversaw initiatives that focused on delivering a crime prevention message to America's youth and youth around the world. Dr. Edwards is currently the President and CEO of Edwards Educational Services, Inc. He also serves as a member of several national and international boards.

Dr. Edwards can be reached at info@realityedservices.com.

Paul E. Chapman, Ph.D.

Dr. Chapman is an associate professor of leadership studies in the College of Human Resources and Education at West Virginia University. His main research interest is public school leadership. He is also engaged in research on character education; 21st-century teaching, learning, and leadership; computer-mediated communication as a pedagogical tool; organizational theory as it applies to school leadership; and teaching techniques for the enhancement of student achievement. Dr. Chapman has published research on the building blocks for preparing good educational leaders, improving retention rates in biochemistry, cohort culture, and educational administration student perceptions of instructional delivery formats. He has been invited to speak and present both nationally and internationally at places like the 13th Annual Character Education Conference, Washington, D. C.; Exeter College, University of Oxford, England; and the College of Science, Technology, and Agriculture of Trinidad and Tobago. Dr. Chapman is a musician and avid fly fisherman.

Dr. Chapman can be reached at PEChapman@mail.wvu.edu.

PREFACE

Society today is changing at a pace that one could not have even imagined just a few short years ago. The pace of change is an inevitable consequence of global conditions and the human quest to know more and do more. Those who will rise as leaders of the future are the ones who find opportunity in an ever-changing world. As Conners, Smith, and Hickman (1994) wrote, successful leaders need to continually ask, *"What else can I do to rise above my circumstances and achieve the results I desire?"*

There are fundamental core elements that contribute to the success of any organization. Schools are no exception. The goal of this book is to explain, examine, and interpret principles that help create a successful school. We call these principles the Six Pillars of Dynamic Schools. Throughout the book, we use stories to provide illustrations of how the Six Pillars can improve practice. It is our hope that these anecdotes will serve as a source of motivation and inspiration, while also providing a little humor.

The Six Pillars focus on *how* we do business rather than *what* business we do. By addressing key concepts within the organizational structure, the Six Pillars can provide positive and measurable outcomes for schools and other organizations. Organizations that make a commitment to building a leadership infrastructure that first focuses on getting the right people and then creating the conditions that enable those people to do their best will be better able to meet the needs of those they serve. In schools, students can only learn in a caring environment that fosters learning. Schools that commit to getting the right people working with our children and creating an organizational structure for positive change can be schools where all students succeed.

As with most books, it is best to read this book cover to cover first in order to get an overview of all six pillars and an understanding of the key principles behind each one. While you are reading, think about how you might use the Six Pillars to strengthen teacher leadership in your school. A key to developing your school as a professional learning community is providing opportunities for teachers to step back from the daily hubbub and reflect on important themes such as relationships and communication. Discussions that focus on the Six Pillars can help do this.

After the first run-through, we recommend that the reader go back and revisit the Six Pillars individually. Although there is a natural and logical connection between the Six Pillars, each section of the book can be used as a stand-alone unit, depending on one's experience, needs, or interests.

As every organization is unique, it is critical to consider how each of the Six Pillars applies to your particular setting. We're confident that you'll be able to apply each of the pillars and the associated principles to any educational setting, regardless of the students' ages or the school's location. Since the Six Pillars transcend socioeconomic class, ethnicity, and cultural background, they also apply to schools in urban, suburban, and rural communities. What's important is the process.

INTRODUCTION:

THE CONTEXT FOR CHANGE

"When you come to the fork in the road, take it."
—Yogi Berra

Education in America is at a crossroads. The accountability movement that has held sway for the last 2 decades, expressed at the national level in the 2001 federal No Child Left Behind (NCLB) Act, defines success in education as every student reaching an established academic benchmark at a specific time. But practitioners know that children come to schools with varying skills, talents, and backgrounds. Moreover, a standardized education will never prepare students for the complex world they will face in the 21st century.

Awareness of the need for a new direction in U.S. education is not new. John Goodlad's *Facing the Future: Issues in Education and Schooling* was published in 1976. In it, Goodlad poses four basic assumptions about schooling for the future:

- First, it is extremely difficult to predict the kinds of behavior that will be most useful for shaping and living in tomorrow's world and which, therefore, should be cultivated in students today.

- Second, the self-renewing individual probably will require proficiency in a talent developed for its own rather than for any overtly utilitarian sake—as well as a breadth of knowledge and skills to cope with the vast array of diverse problems and pressures inherent in modern life.

- Third, if we value humankind, we must always be preoccupied with developing individuals who possess a sense of being, identity, and worth.

- Fourth, it is no longer simply difficult to select and package for instruction the few most important bits and pieces of knowledge—it is impossible (pp. 3-4).

Goodlad wrote, "Perhaps the most disquieting element of all today is uncertainty about the place of education and the role of the schools in a society that can put men on the moon but cannot solve the problems of poverty, pollution, and war" (p. 5). Although he espoused these beliefs 30 years ago, they still apply to schools and schooling today.

That's why the need for visionary leadership in education has never been greater. The visionary leader understands how the past has shaped the present while using creative thought to envision the future through a positive, hopeful lens. Before delving into the heart of this book—the Six Pillars of Dynamic Schools that provide the foundation for visionary leadership for today's schools—let's look briefly at the national trends that have shaped school reform in the recent past and the international trends shaping the challenges of the present and the future in which our students will need to live and thrive.

Where We Are and How We Got Here: The National Perspective

American schooling has always existed in a state of reform. This reform revolves around four basic questions: (a) *What should be taught?* (b) *How should it be taught?* (c) *Who should teach it?* and (d) *Why do we do things the way we do?* School leaders who want to have a lasting impact need to focus on this fourth question, which is the pivotal question for all visionary school reform.

Unfortunately, the advent of NCLB prompted school leaders to turn their focus away from asking the "why?" questions. Instead, all eyes and efforts were focused on a single key performance indicator: test scores. No one can argue with the stated principle of NCLB, that all children deserve the best education possible so they can compete in a global society and have a decent standard of living. But the methods by which federal policy makers decided to reach this goal were flawed because they have been based on more than 50 years of blame-the-schools mentality, as described below.

The 1950s. The launching of *Sputnik* by the Soviet Union in 1957 propelled us into an era of accelerated change that, until that point, had not been matched in the history of humankind. The Cold War had taken a new turn, and American educators were asked to respond. Political leaders responded to *Sputnik* by challenging the education system to raise standards in mathematics and science. But there was a more lasting impact: Bracey (2009) contends that, with the launch of *Sputnik*, most Americans blamed our schools for failing to educate students and felt that this was the major reason the Russians had jumped ahead in the race for space. American educators have been taking it on the chin ever since. Every new wave of reform and major shift in thinking about how schools should work since then has begun with the notion that they don't.

Other changes in American society during this period also had profound effects on education. Since the end of World War II, the United States had enjoyed a prosperous lifestyle and a booming economy that afforded jobs and opportunities for countless citizens, with or without a high school diploma. But that was ending—young people would need, at minimum, a high school education with specific marketable skills beyond secondary schooling if they wished to remain competitive in the workforce. For the first time, the measure of success for U.S. schools would be getting all students to graduate high school.

The 1950s also saw the Civil Rights Movement, which would transform the nation and the education establishment. Although legal segregation ended during that period, our education system made only minimal gains with respect to real desegregation. Today, schools in urban areas are still predominantly composed of children of color while many suburbs and rural communities remain predominantly White. Inequities in educational quality and stubborn achievement gaps based on race/ethnicity and socioeconomic status continue to be major challenges and are the focus of school reform.

Every new wave of reform and major shift in thinking about how schools should work has begun with the notion that they don't.

The 1960s and 1970s. Challenges to the American education system continued through the next 2 decades. The Vietnam War and the social revolution of the 1960s and 1970s raised questions about the establishment. Change from a conservative social structure to a liberal, more questioning approach influenced schools, which began to broaden their curricula to meet a changing social framework. Throughout the 1970s, open campuses, student walkouts, and sit-ins protesting everything from cafeteria food to school policies and curricula became common. Youth were responding to the changing times, and schools were forced to adjust.

As the postwar baby boom of the early 1970s increased the number of school-age children, communities felt the impact of a shortage of schools and teachers. Split sessions to accommodate overcrowding became the norm; this, combined with an energy crisis, placed a further burden on schools. Schools made use of creative scheduling techniques to meet the needs of students. Modular scheduling, as opposed to the more traditional 40- to 50-minute class periods, became popular. However, this form of scheduling was complex and cumbersome for both staff and students.

The 1980s. This decade brought heightened criticisms of the quality of American schools. The release of the national report *A Nation at Risk* in 1983 pointed out inadequacies of the nation's education system, and subsequent reports continued to focus on shortcomings. The education community was faced with a need to address learning standards and accountability. Reformers began to move away from the student-centered, personalized approaches of the 1970s and toward a more standardized approach. Many states adopted standards for curriculum content and implemented state-wide mandates to make the standards the basis of all content to be delivered. Mechanisms for measuring whether or not students were learning these basic curriculum content elements would soon follow.

The 1990s. As states continued to expand standards and account-ability, a new reform challenge arose—the question of school safe-ty. Events such as the tragic shootings at Columbine, Jonesboro, and Paducah raised the nation's consciousness and brought school safety into question. Further contributing to the drama was the fact that many of these events took place in suburban America, where school safety had been taken for granted. In urban school settings, incidents of school violence had been the norm for years and, sadly, were almost accepted. Yet the shift of school violence to suburbia raised the level of consciousness and brought school safety to the forefront of the national agenda.

The 1990s was also a decade focused on exploring new and different options to the more traditional public education model. At the fed-eral level, the *Goals 2000* initiative committed the nation to excel-lence in public education in a variety of academic and nonacademic fronts. Vouchers, charter schools, and privatization were products of the 1990s, gaining limited success in pockets across the country and demonstrating a lack of confidence in public education.

Into the 21st century. The last decade has seen the continuation of these reform forces—most notably the tendency to look to schools for solutions to society's ills and the goal of raising achievement for all students through common standards and accountability. These mind-sets reached their ultimate expression in the passage of NCLB. But as we'll see in the following section, this perspective is not sufficient to lead us into the challenges of the 21st century.

WHERE WE'RE GOING AND WHERE WE NEED TO GO: THE GLOBAL PERSPECTIVE

All around us, forward-looking thinkers are proclaiming that the 21st century demands leadership with a global perspective. In his book *The World is Flat: A Brief History of the 21st Century,* Friedman (2006) describes an international world economy with players who can compete in a global sense, regardless of place, space, and time. Friedman outlines 10 geopolitical events, innovations, and companies that have brought about a world economy that is no longer an exclusive club. At the end of the day, any small-business operator or large-corporation CEO who does not place an international lens in his or her toolbox of operational guidance will not succeed.

Education leaders are bound by the same rules of competition as other organizational leaders. Yong Zhao (2008), a distinguished professor and executive director of the Confucius Institute at Michigan State University, often presents to business and education leaders. In his presentation, he contends that educational institutions and solvent businesses around the world evolve continuously; one of the driving forces in this evolution is global economic competitiveness, and no innovative leader can afford to think otherwise.

Walter C. Clemens (2000), a professor at Boston University, presents six possibilities for the future of global society:

- In the first scenario, *Unipolar Stability*, the U.S. maintains a
  single superpower status, but uses strong business alliances
  for mutual growth and prosperity. Economic growth for
  most of the world traders is steady and shared. The world
  remains a peaceful place, for the most part.

- In scenario two, *Fragmented Chaos*, the relative calm and
  stability for the affluent traders of the world is shattered by
  the failing of the earth's biosphere and the outpouring of violence perpetuated by the world's downtrodden. Diseases run
  rampant on a global scale and weapons of mass destruction
  fall into the hands of many desperate enough to use them.
  Courageous leadership is not to be found, and democracy
  falls into decline globally.

- The third scenario, *Challenge to the Hegemon*, paints the U.S.
  as the declining state challenged by a rising China, which
  bullies its neighbors unchecked and builds up for a major
  confrontation with the U.S. that it thinks it will win.

- The fourth scenario, *Bipolar Cooperation*, depicts a world
  where the U.S. and China exist symbiotically. There is cooperation between and among the social and economic sectors, to the benefit of the people. Politics are overridden by
  recognition of collaborative growth for both countries.

- Scenario five, *Multipolar Cooperation*, presents a view where the domino effect for democracy takes hold, and peace is a byproduct of countries wanting to grow by participating in the global market.

- The final scenario, *Global Governance Without World Government*, gives rise to Non-Governmental Organizations (NGOs) that work in cooperation with world governments to fulfill human needs. As human needs are met by this collaboration, economic growth and prosperity reach many who previously did not have a good standard of life.

Which of these scenarios comes to pass will be influenced by how well we adjust to globalization—and that depends on how well we educate our citizens to adapt to global trends. Norman R. Augustine (2008), retired chairman and CEO of Lockheed Martin Corporation and winner of the Public Welfare Medal in 2006, contends that the U.S. will "fall off the *Flat Earth*" if we continue to educate people the way we have for the last 100 years (p. 8).

The forces of change will become greater as society moves at a more rapid pace. The challenges to compete in an ever-shrinking world will continue to test our creativity and our ability to address change in the education community.

Four Macro Trends

Another way to look at the challenges facing education leaders is to consider four macro trends shaping modern life: *Globalization, Localization, Digitalization,* and *Fragmentation.* These are the guideposts for setting a vision, because each macro trend manifests itself as a driver of change.

Globalization

We have already touched on macro trend number one, *globalization,* the result of society's embrace of the information age and the Internet, which allows people to access knowledge and connect with one another from any point on earth (Friedman, 2006). That immediate access allows people around the world to participate on the world stage.

Localization

The macro trend of globalization leads to the second trend, *localization.* Because of globalization, the world is smaller than its actual size in relation to any town, city, state, nation, or region. People can communicate instantly with one another from almost any point on earth via the Internet. Organizations, or even individuals, have the ability to seek out and find others who hold similar views and values.

Localization may occur virtually when individuals of the same mind-set and sensibilities form a subculture that is real in every way other than the physical. It can also lead to face-to-face physical contacts and experiences. For example, the Appalachian region of the United States has many towns that celebrate ancestral heritage from the Celtic traditions. Any small town that creates a Web page can tell the connected world of a weeklong Highlands celebration, and people from all over the globe with an interest in that subculture have the opportunity to go and actually participate in the celebration. Still others may choose to participate in the virtual arena. In either case, localization allows subcultures to build and maintain an identity limited only by imagination. These identities are real and give people feelings of self-worth and connectedness.

Digitalization

The Pew Global Attitudes Project (2006) found that "Internet use is on the rise in both industrialized societies and developing countries, with the greatest increases among the British, Poles and French" (p. 3). All indications are that the world is becoming more connected. How does this factor into our relationships with people? This is the question that the third macro trend, *digitalization,* raises.

The virtual world is boundless in terms of the global perspective. The more people become connected to both the World Wide Web and one another, the more they value technology and the relationships it fosters. Web users value their virtual relationships much like people of small communities value sitting on the front porch chatting with neighbors. For many, the Web is the new front porch. The idea that there are just a few degrees of separation between any two people has been transformed—now, it's just **one** degree of separation.

Fragmentation

The fourth macro trend, *fragmentation,* is the driving force behind the diversification of all aspects of our lives. During the 20th century, great strides were made in global communications, such as oceanic cable lines and wireless telecommunications. Even with these improvements, it was still quite easy to find small towns, cities, nations, and regions where there was some homogeneity in thought and views. In the 21st century, the Internet's advancement in global communications has had a splintering effect on local popular cultures.

Toffler (1990) holds that the demassification of the airwaves has led to the breakup of mass audiences into segments and subgroups, which gives people a broader range of choices in developing their self-images. Meanwhile, the Internet allows individuals to choose how they will impart their self-image to others.

People now have an abundance of lives and cultures from which to choose, and many choose to participate in more than one subculture. The hidden subcultures among us are too numerous to identify. They can be likened to the iceberg that shows only 20% of its structure above the surface of the water.

The Courage to Respond to the Trends

"Courage is the thing. All goes if courage goes."
— Sir James Matthew Barrie

The trends described by the thinkers and futurists cited here, as well as many others, are dynamic forces shaping the interactions between all economic, geopolitical, and cultural groups. To ignore these forces means we all lose on the grandest of scales. Whether the need is to provide equal opportunity through education, provide health care for all, or feed the hungry, seeing people of the world as isolated pockets of humanity is no longer a viable paradigm.

In Stephen Covey's groundbreaking book, *The Seven Habits of Highly Effective People* (1989), he wrote, "Renewal is the principle—and the process—that empowers us to move on an upward spiral of growth and change, of continuous improvement" (p. 304). Courageous leaders, by their actions and words, have the ability to move people to do things that they otherwise would never have contemplated. Leaders accomplish this by sharing a vision of the future and collaborating with others to solve the myriad of global issues we face.

Yet, schools have historically resisted change. The unwritten policy has been to be reactive rather than proactive. Although changes in society have been dramatic and are ever-evolving, only minimal modifications have been made to daily school schedules and curricula. In many ways, current curricular offerings and student schedules are consistent with the offerings of decades ago.

"There is . . . a remarkable consensus among educators and business and policy leaders on one key conclusion: we need to bring what we teach and how we teach into the 21st Century" (Wallis, 2006).

How to Bring Our Schools Out of the 20th Century

Schools are not atypical; most organizations and individuals traditionally resist change. After all, the first rule of physics is that a body at rest tends to remains at rest. Yet, imagine if non-educational organizations had resisted change to the extent that schools have. The ability to recognize change, embrace it, and be proactive is a hallmark of a successful organization. The most successful companies today are not doing business the same way they did 50 years ago.

The same is true for the most successful schools in America. They have embraced change, against tremendous odds in many cases. We see pockets of outstanding schools across the country that have raised academic standards and have created safe and caring learning environments for their students. Leaders of such schools understand the dynamic nature of international, national, and local events and how they affect teaching and learning. These leaders are able to influence school culture so that adaptability to changing conditions becomes standard operating procedure.

The ability to recognize change, embrace it, and be proactive is a hallmark of a successful organization.

Schools are complex organizations that are challenged daily to meet the needs of an intricate and ever-changing population, and they must demonstrate the flexibility to continually meet the needs of their students. School leaders who understand global circumstances and conditions are more likely to develop a vision of what content and pedagogy will produce graduates capable of competing in a global economy. The vision may have its beginnings as a leader's solitary thought, but it can only become reality through collaboration.

The Six Pillars: A Framework for Collaborating for Change

Building and sustaining collaboration for reform that responds to the needs of the 21st century is the focus of the Six Pillars of Dynamic Schools that are the heart of this book. These pillars are:

1. Communication and relationships
2. Leadership and empowerment
3. Planning and evaluation
4. Collaboration
5. Accountability and responsibility
6. Consistency and redundancy

Each of the Six Pillars maintains a thematic focus that individuals or groups can work on. If a person or a group makes a commitment to improve and concentrates on the Six Pillars, amazing things will happen.

The next section will explore how the Six Pillars were developed through the reform process at a school much like many others that are in urgent need of change, and the remainder of this book will look at each of the Six Pillars in more depth. But first, to get started in thinking about how the Six Pillars can combine with the trends discussed in this introduction to produce maximum influence on the culture and change process, consider Table 1.1. Look, for example, at some of the ways the pillar of *communication and relationships* intersects with the four macro trends:

- Globalization—Build collaborations with people who are skilled in finding and using knowledge.

- Localization—Share the wealth of problems solved and progress made.

- Digitalization—Seek out, reframe, and articulate multiple perspectives salient to your causes.

- Fragmentation—Work, celebrate, and be with people regularly.

When the four macro trends are used as a context for leaders' work *and* the Six Pillars are used as a guide for thinking, doing, and communicating, a leader's influence on organizational culture becomes a powerful force for positive change. Table 1.1 elaborates on the intersections of the macro trends and the Six Pillars.

Table 1.1 *The Six Pillars in the context of the Four Macro Trends*

The Six Pillars	The Four Macro Trends	
	Globalization	*Localization*
Communication and Relationships	• Convey a message about use of knowledge and how it is accessed. (We can find the answers that will help us because we will find them together. All questions are answerable and all problems are solvable.) • Build collaborations with people who are skilled in finding and using knowledge.	• Export the organizational culture via technological tools. • Expand Problem-Based Collaboration Teams to include locals from around the world. • Share the wealth of problems solved and progress made.
Leadership and Empowerment	• Model the way in use of technology tools for work. • Celebrate with and allow those who have skill with and knowledge of new technologies enjoy their accomplishments.	• Enable all members of the organization to be connected and included. • Encourage members of the organization to show pride in the collaborative culture.
Planning and Evaluation	• Keep up with and use new technology tools to plan and evaluate work. (Consider only tools that make work easier and more enjoyable.)	• Plan together, play together, and persevere through the hard times by giving support to others. • Evaluate what is important for strengthening the local identity.
Collaboration	• Consider the real problems of the work and build a culture of collaboration to solve them (ex., Problem-Based Collaboration Teams).	• Continually define the unique aspects of the organizational culture that strengthen individual and group identity.
Accountability and Responsibility	• Choose professional and personal growth in terms of keeping up with useful technology tools and expect others to do the same.	• Be responsible for identification of how successful organizational methods and goals are shared and demonstrate accountability to all stakeholders by sharing.
Consistency and Redundancy	• Stay on message about getting better every day and enjoying the work.	• Stay connected and help others get connected on a personal level with current and new technology.

Table 1.1 *The Six Pillars* in the context of the *Four Macro Trends (Continued)*

The Six Pillars	The Four Macro Trends	
	Digitalization	*Fragmentation*
Communication and Relationships	• Model reaching out across the Web for building collaboration teams and relationships. • Seek out, reframe, and articulate multiple perspectives salient to your causes.	• Work, celebrate, and be with people regularly. • Set up work spaces for different types of work habits. • Play should be part of work and learning.
Leadership and Empowerment	• Empower others to take risks concerning global relationship building and reward success. • Share your own successes in terms of expanding and growing the organization via virtual teaming.	• Encourage stakeholders to see the symbolic nature of what the organization does. • Reward creativity.
Planning and Evaluation	• Plan with the virtual world at the forefront of your strategic thinking. • Evaluate the innovative strategies based on project-by-project success and overall organizational growth.	• Plan with an understanding that no one image of a subculture or a person can cover the diversity that lies within.
Collaboration	• Collaborate with stakeholders across the globe via the Web.	• Use symbols to extend greetings and invitations of inquiry about what the organization does.
Accountability and Responsibility	• Set personal goals to think outside of the box when in comes to technology use and test ideas with stakeholder groups (ex., I will test two new ideas a week). • Be responsible for finding better ways to do things.	• Search for, find, and build up the core of every person by getting to know and understand who they really are.
Consistency and Redundancy	• Stay focused on improvement of work and service and keep modeling.	• Stay true to yourself regardless of pressure from other people.

EVOLUTION OF THE SIX PILLARS: ONE SCHOOL'S CHANGE STORY

"The difficult we do immediately; the impossible might
take a little longer."
—Motto of the U.S. Army Corps of Engineers during World War II

No two schools attempt to reach their goals the same way—nor should they. One size does not fit all. Each institution has its own unique personality based on the many individuals who make up the school community. When these individuals come together and work to accomplish something with a single-minded purpose, their bonds to one another become stronger. The stronger the bonds become, the deeper the entrenchment of core values. These values become the basis for how things get done. And how things get done becomes the culture.

Consider what happened at East Hartford High School (East Hartford, CT), where one of us, Steve, served as principal from 1992 to 2002. An aircraft engine manufacturing plant that had employed more than 30,000 workers in the school's urban community in the 1960s now employed fewer than 1,000; this change had a dramatic impact on the school. Workers and their families moved to other towns, the tax base decreased, housing prices dropped, crime increased, and the quality of life in the neighborhoods around the school steadily declined. The school also witnessed an increase in crime and disruptive behavior within its walls. Once that began to happen, student attendance, motivation, and achievement suffered. What follows is Steve's story.

When I arrived as principal in the fall of 1992, to say that this school was dysfunctional would have been an understatement. The same principal had been at the school for the previous 17 years, and any change initiatives that had been attempted had long since stalled. The school was on autopilot and losing altitude. Drop-out and retention rates (especially in 9th grade) were increasing, SAT scores were falling, and behavioral incidents were steadily on the rise. Although these indicators were there, few people, if any, took notice.

With conditions in the school bordering on dangerous, the staff began to operate in isolation, thus contributing little to the health of the organization at large. Teachers had no sense of collective purpose. Feeling helpless to improve the school as a whole, teachers focused on maintaining safety and security within their classrooms, the familiar environment in which they felt most comfortable. One teacher told me that he could not control the school, but he could control his classroom. I responded that, although this may be true for the short term, his classroom walls would not protect him if the school continued to decline.

On my first day as principal, I noticed the school district's framed mission statement hanging on the wall in the main lobby. I began to ask teachers questions about the mission statement: when had it last been updated, how they were attempting to fulfill the mission statement, and even what it was. Although several people made guesses, no one seemed to know the answers. The history, and even existence, of the mission statement was a mystery to the staff.

Core values become the basis for how things get done. And how things get done becomes the culture.

Further investigation revealed that the mission statement was a result of a districtwide strategic planning session that had taken place more than 5 years before, involving only a few representatives from each of the schools in the district. Although intentions were good, this process created no sense of staff ownership. Without a clearly defined and articulated mission, there was no sense of direction. Imagine a number of vectors on a diagram all pointing in different directions with no semblance of order (see Figure 1.1). Ideally a series of vectors should operate independently, yet point in the same direction, with a common sense of purpose (see Figure 1.2). Here, staff members felt a lack of ownership in the mission of the school. There was no sense of collective purpose; the only commonality was that all teachers were housed in the same physical structure, in classrooms with students.

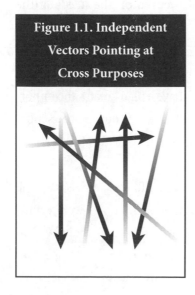

Figure 1.1. Independent Vectors Pointing at Cross Purposes

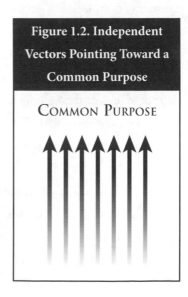

Figure 1.2. Independent Vectors Pointing Toward a Common Purpose

Furthermore, the staff had no way of knowing how to measure success. How would they know whether they were following the mission? How would they know whether they had reached established goals? Was East Hartford High's success based on a particular percentage of students who met a predetermined score on a state assessment instrument? Or on the percentage of students who graduated?

If there is no sense of collective purpose in a school, the only commonality is that all teachers are housed in the same physical structure, in classrooms with students.

I knew that, if our school staff was going to be able to document positive movement, we would have to articulate a vision that incorporated a mission to establish clear and measurable outcomes with respect to student achievement and social and emotional development. Such a vision could only be developed through commitment to a planning process that focused on the needs of the populations the school served.

Time was of the essence; the school had no direction, no clearly defined vision, and no plan. Failure to have a plan creates the opportunity for someone else to come up with one for you, and the school was on the verge of having someone from the outside take over.

It was clear that a total organizational shift was necessary—the vectors needed to be realigned so that all staff efforts were pointed in the same direction. However, it was also clear that it would be neither swift nor easy. Historically, people resist change. Beyond the anticipated resistance, it was also clear that a change initiative of this magnitude required time—a 3- to 5-year commitment. The first step would be to create an organizational structure that embraced change, and the second step would be to foster commitment to a process to *sustain* the organizational growth.

Failure to have a plan creates the opportunity for someone else to come up with one for you.

Based on a strategic planning process, the staff and I identified East Hartford High's specific needs—the elements that we believed were crucial for improving student performance and the climate of the school. When we examined the data and looked closely at the school's student population, the same themes surfaced repeatedly. These themes were later identified as the Six Pillars of Dynamic Schools:

- Communication and relationships
- Leadership and empowerment
- Planning and evaluation
- Collaboration
- Accountability and responsibility
- Consistency and redundancy

Together, we made a commitment to implement each of the Six Pillars. The result was significant; over time, we reduced the dropout rate, had fewer suspensions and retentions, and increased academic performance and overall student success. By addressing the Six Pillars simultaneously, we were able to attack problems on multiple fronts. And, together, we achieved success, as this quote from a report issued by the Connecticut Institute of Municipal Studies (1998) demonstrates:

The place to visit is East Hartford High School which has become an acknowledged model of innovation, coordination of resources, and programs…the combination develops a strong sense of community, where no student is allowed to fail.…East Hartford High School's SAT and CAP test scores have risen every year and are now among the highest in the state's 14 urban districts. Both suspensions and student fighting are down more than 50 percent despite significant enrollment increases. (p.12)

How One Change Can Have Broad Effects

The change process is affected by countless variables. A change in one area may positively or negatively affect other areas, and the more complex the organization, the more variables that must be considered when implementing change. Authors of the report issued by the Connecticut Institute of Municipal Studies (1998) talk about this:

Educators and others who've seen these numbers always ask Edwards for his secret, the one magic thing he's doing that no one else is doing. "There isn't any one thing," he says…. But if there is one thing, Edwards supposes it's that he and his staff know the kids.

To illustrate this idea, let's look at just one of the changes made at East Hartford High. Passing time—the 5 minutes between classes—is a discipline challenge at many secondary schools. Releasing 2,400 teenagers into a hallway at one time dramatically increases the potential for incidents among students to occur. Our staff wanted to look at creative ways to analyze and minimize incidents during passing time.

After building relationships and trust with many faculty members, I put a problem-solving team (PST) together. The team first focused on the 6-minute homeroom period at the beginning of the day, during which attendance was taken and information was distributed to students. At the end of the 6-minute homeroom period, students had a 5-minute passing time to go to their first-period class. Looking at this schedule, the PST realized that, by combining the homeroom period with the students' first-period class, they could eliminate one of the passing times, thus reducing the opportunity for incidents to take place, decreasing tardiness to first period, and increasing instructional time. Saving 5 minutes per day during a 180-day school year equates to 20 45-minute class periods. This change would clearly have a positive impact on safety and instructional time.

As with any new initiative, combining first period and homeroom met some initial staff resistance. Formerly, homerooms had always been grouped by grade. At first, some teachers complained that combining homeroom and first period now mixed kids from different grades together. How would students in different grades get the information they needed? The school's guidance director solved this situation by identifying students in each period by grade; when information needed to get out to students based on their grade, the appropriate number of papers could be placed in each teacher's mailbox for distribution the next day.

Once staff concerns were addressed and the change was implemented, it became clear to the entire school that, in this case, the positives far outweighed the negatives. Ultimately, making this one small modification had substantial positive repercussions in the daily lives of students. Adding 5 minutes of instructional time per day may not sound like much, but the cumulative impact was significant.

Creating the PST and implementing a change increasing class time (even by only 5 minutes a day) utilized many of the Six Pillars. The PST empowered teachers to take on a leadership role that would allow them to work with a broader spectrum of school staff and make a decision that would impact the structure of the school day. The PST had to collaborate in the planning and evaluation of their decision. They knew that this decision would have ramifications because it challenged the status quo; it went against "the way things have always been done."

Challenging the status quo is a characteristic of second-order change. Second-order change is not linear; it is change that does not typically have a clear pathway, so the outcome is often unclear. Change of this type opens the door for other change initiatives. First-order change is an extension of the known; it is usually linear and has a predictable outcome. It does not move people outside of their comfort zone, which is why second-order change can often be more challenging.

As part of its role, the PST needed to communicate the process and ultimate decision to the entire faculty and staff. They were accountable for that decision and took collective responsibility for it. When teams of professionals within the organization have the opportunity to play a role in the decision-making process, they feel a greater sense of ownership for the school and the decision.

Making one small modification in a school's routine can have substantial positive repercussions in the daily lives of students.

CAUTION: EVERY SCHOOL IS DIFFERENT

The Six Pillars of Dynamic Schools are the key elements for implementing a successful organizational growth initiative. Furthermore, the pillars are critical to sustaining continuous school improvement. In order to truly achieve success, however, the process must be institutionalized and owned by the entire school staff as an embedded feature of the organization's culture. Thus, any successful change process explicitly recognizes that the school's context—its needs, strengths, and history—needs to be taken into account.

Over the years, countless school leaders visited East Hartford High to observe our school's interdisciplinary teaching team model in practice. Many of them were able to implement similar models at their school settings. However, these successes were the result of the visiting leaders connecting with only those ideas that most benefited their school's specific nuances.

One spring, a team of teachers and administrators visited the school to learn about the interdisciplinary teaching team model. They spent 1 day visiting team teachers, observing classes, meeting with administrators, and talking with students. During my conversations with them, I cautioned that our model had been specifically designed to meet the needs of our students. Changes had not taken place overnight—in fact, the entire interdisciplinary team teaching model was implemented over a 4-year period—and throughout the process, we gave careful attention to creating staff ownership. Knowing that staff development and training was critical to prepare teachers for working in this type of educational setting, I retained the services of a noted educational teaming consultant, who worked closely with the staff and administration for 2 years to present current research that validated the concept and assisted in translating research into practice in building the teaming model.

Public education is a complex system; examining only one variable not only limits the impact of any change effort, it may in fact create an imbalance.

I emphasized to the school visitors that implementing the interdisciplinary teaching team model was a process, not a solution in and of itself. It would take time, training, and staff ownership to implement such a large-scale initiative successfully.

After that 1 day, the visiting team left and I did not hear from them again until the following October. The school principal called to tell me that they had implemented the interdisciplinary teaching team model in their school, and it was failing miserably. Teachers had rejected the concept, and neither parents nor students had bought into the new model. The staff had lost confidence in the principal, who in turn had lost confidence in his ability to lead. Although his motives were honorable, his plan was faulty. He had attempted to replicate one school's successful program in his own building without modifying it to meet the specific needs of his population and adapting it to the context of his environment and local community.

The Forces of Change

Looking at the Six Pillars, it is hard to imagine one without the other five. As was discussed earlier, public education is a complex system; examining only one variable not only limits the impact of any change effort, it may in fact create an imbalance. Multiple forces exist within any organization: driving forces push for change and opposing forces resist change. When the forces are in balance, a state of equilibrium exists and the organization remains stagnant. Such organizations in equilibrium have reached a plateau—which, in reality, is a move backward. Successful organizations avoid this state of complacency by constantly reinventing themselves.

There are several ways to do this, if one understands the forces at work: by strengthening driving forces, by reducing or weakening the resisting forces, or by working on both sides of the equation at the same time.

The following example illustrates the concept of opposing forces at work in schools. Assume that scores on the Scholastic Aptitude Test (SAT) have had a slight but steady decline at your school over the past several years. Both math and verbal scores are now below the state and national average. There are a number of driving forces at play that are pushing for a change in this condition. On the other side of the equation, there are resisting forces that are countering the change effort to increase SAT scores (see Figure 1.3).

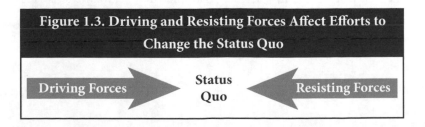

Figure 1.3. Driving and Resisting Forces Affect Efforts to Change the Status Quo

Driving Forces → Status Quo ← Resisting Forces

There are many possible driving forces for our example (i.e., efforts to improve SAT scores). Some of these might include:

- Pressure from central administration
- Media attention
- Concerns shared by the Parent-Teacher Organization
- Concerns raised by college admissions personnel

Resisting forces also exist, however, that can create a state of equilibrium. These might include:

- Faculty who see the SATs as an add-on, with state testing driving the curriculum
- Decline in number of students taking the Preliminary SAT (PSAT)
- Significant number of students who are not taking algebra or geometry until their junior year of high school

The state of equilibrium created by a balance of the driving and resisting forces essentially prevents any substantial change from taking place, although the end result of a lack of movement may be a steady decline in SAT scores. To create positive action, either the driving forces must be strengthened, the resisting forces must be weakened, or the school must do a combination of both (i.e., work on strengthening the driving forces while weakening the resisting forces at the same time). Figure 1.4 lists possible examples of how the resisting forces in our SAT example may be weakened. This emphasizes the importance of clearly identifying resisting forces and spending time thinking about ways to address each of them.

Figure 1.4. Addressing Driving and Resisting Forces to Create Positive Action

STRENGTHENING DRIVING FORCES

- Engage central administration in problem solving and make use of their resources for data collection and analysis
- Have the media do a story on new initiatives that have been put in place to address declining scores
- Engage the Parent-Teacher Organization as an ally in promoting test preparation
- Develop a stronger relationship with area colleges and strategize on ways to enhance students' SAT scores

WEAKENING RESISTING FORCES

- Establish a faculty SAT task force that includes some of the naysayers to examine where SAT preparation could fit into existing curriculum
- Require all juniors to take the PSAT
- Realign the school's mathematics program to better meet the needs of college-bound students

Each of the Six Pillars in this book can be viewed as a driving force and, for each of these pillars, multiple resisting forces exist. A thorough analysis of any organizational growth effort will lead to the identification of these opposing forces. By looking at organizational growth from both perspectives, we create greater opportunity for change to occur.

CHAPTER ONE

PILLAR ONE:
COMMUNICATION AND
RELATIONSHIPS

"Children may not remember what you taught them, but they will
always remember how you treated them."
—Author unknown

"It's not about sophisticated pedagogy; it's all about relationships."
—Asa Hilliard

In *Lincoln on Leadership: Executive Strategies for Tough Times,* Donald Phillips (1992) describes Abraham Lincoln's commanding communication skills. Lincoln never used coercion as a tactic to persuade others. "He was poised and confident under pressure, and he influenced others with his friendly manner, openness, and verbal skills" (p. 38).

This chapter shows how school administrators and teachers can, like Lincoln, hone their communication skills to build lasting, meaningful relationships and motivate people to achieve great things. First, we tell two stories of principals who understand the value of communication when building relationships of trust and respect. The first, Sylvia, turned negative recognition into positive recognition to reach out to some aspiring student-artists in her school, which ultimately helped change an entire school and community culture for the better. The second, Mary, demonstrated that respect does not mean avoiding conflict; it can also be expressed by directness and firmness. Next, we discuss the process of building and sustaining lasting relationships based on personalization. Finally, we consider how relationship building can help in dealing with staff members who resist change and with students whose behavior keeps them from achieving their potential.

HARNESSING THE ENERGY OF THE GRAFFITI ARTIST

Sylvia was a young principal who took over at an urban high school, where she noticed a significant problem with graffiti in and around the building. It was evident that there were some talented artists among her students who were funneling their artistic talents in the wrong way. Sylvia's first strategy was to make sure the graffiti was always removed as soon as possible, but of course this became a game with the "taggers"; as soon as the graffiti disappeared, a new and even more elaborate piece of art would take its place the next day.

Sylvia knew that she had entered a battle of wills and that removing the graffiti was only a short-term fix. The solution to this problem was not to "win" the battle, but to use her communication and relationship-building skills to change the rules.

After Sylvia identified a few of the major "artists," she scheduled a time to meet with each of them individually in her office. The first one was Tao, a short, stocky African American 11th-grader. Tao's manner was cold but respectful. Sylvia greeted Tao with a smile and a handshake, invited him to sit down, and offered him a juice from a small refrigerator she kept in her office. She sat down near Tao and made small talk. "How are your classes going? What are your favorite subjects?" Soon Tao asked Sylvia the inevitable question, "Why am I here?" She replied that she wanted to have the opportunity to meet one of the more talented artists in the school. With a quizzical look, he leaned back in his chair and asked, "Me?" Sylvia said, "Yes, Tao, of course you." She told him that she saw evidence of his artistic ability every morning when she walked into the building, and she mentioned several designs she had particularly enjoyed. A smile came across Tao's face. Clearly, he had rarely received positive recognition for his art.

Sylvia explained to Tao that, although his artwork was excellent, she felt that as the new principal of the school she needed to develop a theme of artwork that flowed throughout the building, rather than random drawings. Resting his head on his chin, Tao began to lean forward in his chair. Sylvia asked him if he had any ideas. He did—so many, in fact, that Sylvia had to write them down on paper to make sure she would not forget any. Sylvia explained that, with a project of this magnitude, she would need more students to help. Tao offered Sylvia the names of several other taggers, and they set a time to convene in the conference room and discuss the project with the school activities coordinator and one of the art teachers.

At the next meeting, it was obvious that Tao had done some background work; he had informed the six other young men at the meeting about the schoolwide art project. Members of the group were excited to participate. For the most part, they had been disengaged from school and were in an adversarial role with teachers and the administration. Just by coming to the meeting, they were forging new ground that set the stage for unlimited possibilities.

One of the group's first suggestions was to change the school's multicolored walls to one uniform color throughout the school. Sylvia thought this was an outstanding suggestion. The group collectively came up with the idea of a "helping hands" day: They recruited students and staff to come in on a Saturday and, under the watchful eyes of the head custodian and Sylvia, painted the hallways. Sylvia persuaded a local hardware store to donate the paint for the project.

Once the hallways were painted, the artists were ready to begin their mural project. They organized into three groups—one to design new murals, another to paint them, and a third to maintain and refurbish them. Sylvia had two requests: one, that she have final say on the mural designs to ensure they were appropriate for a general audience; and two, that all murals be painted in black and yellow, the school colors. At first, the team was resistant to the two-color scheme, but Sylvia explained that it would make it easier for touch-ups, provide consistency from mural to mural, and reduce costs. Finally, they agreed.

All painting was done during the students' free period and after school. Regular announcements over the public address system kept the student body apprised of the progress. After a number of murals had been completed, the school held an open house to showcase the project, inviting families, friends, central-office administrators, the board of education, local dignitaries, and the media. The event, organized by the students, featured live music from the school's jazz band, refreshments from the school's culinary program, and members of the student council acting as tour guides. The artists prepared programs that were then printed by students in the graphic arts department, and each artist stood by his mural to provide viewers with artistic interpretations. Sylvia presented the student artists with plaques for their positive contributions to the school and community.

The student artists and the school received significant print and television media coverage. This event brought positive visibility to a school and to a group of young men who were in desperate need of positive recognition and appreciation. Incidents of graffiti became virtually nonexistent. In addition, the project was the beginning of a cultural shift in the school; for the first time, youth began to trust the adults in the school, and adults and students began to work together for the betterment of the school.

Eleven years later, new murals are being designed and painted by the fourth generation of taggers. The original group passed on their experience to younger students, and the tradition has continued. Although Sylvia has moved on to a new school, the original photograph in which she is standing with Tao and his cousin next to the first mural hangs in her current office. This picture serves as a constant reminder of what school leaders can accomplish when they use communication skills to develop positive relationships with students and build a school climate of respect and trust.

STARTING OFF ON THE RIGHT FOOT

The first days of school always present a challenge. As students arrive, some feel a need to claim their turf or establish their position at the school. This often occurs with students who are new to the building, whether they have transferred from another school or moved up from a lower grade.

Mary knew that, as principal, she was responsible during these first days for setting the tone for the whole year. While she was standing in the main lobby welcoming students as they came off the buses for the first day, Mary noticed a group of boys gathering near the building's main entrance. Each student wore jeans, a white T-shirt, and a red bandana tied around his right ankle. The 12 boys in the group all appeared to be 9th-graders. As Mary approached the group, they quickly dispersed. She radioed security and asked them to bring students who met the description to her conference room. Within 15 minutes, most of the group had been located.

When Mary walked into the conference room, few of the students made eye contact with her; most sat leaning back in their chairs, arms folded across their chests. Mary sat down at the large conference table and welcomed them to the high school. One student quickly spoke up and asked why the group was being detained—since they had done nothing wrong, he said, she had no right to deny them their education. Mary made it clear that it was not her intent to deny them an education; she was simply surprised to see so many students wearing the same outfit, and she was also disturbed that, when she approached the group, they all ran away.

The student stated that they were dressed this way because they were members of the "dog pound"—a club from their neighborhood. Mary expressed concern that, as a group, they gave the appearance of a gang, especially considering their jittery behavior. She indicated that for her peace of mind she needed to resolve this issue; therefore she would be asking each of their parents to come in and discuss the matter.

Fortunately, Mary was able to get in touch with most of the parents, and they were willing and able to immediately come to the school to meet with her. She brought them into the conference room with their sons and explained the situation. The parents expressed surprise that their sons had all left for school wearing the same outfits. They took each of their sons home to change and then brought them back to school. Before the parents left, Mary spent some time speaking with them alone about the importance of the school and the parents working together to meet their children's needs.

In this example, Mary showed respect in a different way than Sylvia did with her graffiti artists. She treated the students like the young adults they were, but she did not skirt the issue of the inappropriate way they had dressed and acted. She was direct and spoke plainly about the issue head-on, while maintaining a respectful tone and words. Mary took the same approach with the parents, and the resulting relationships became strong and positive. By showing respect for others and modeling trustworthiness, Mary opened up the two-way communication that resulted in the positive outcome.

From Recognition to Personalization

Positive communication and relationships should be the foundation of all we do with students. Without establishing positive relationships with our students, we will merely be the delivery system for curriculum. In a 5-year study involving 10,000 students, James and Ciurczak (2004) found that a significant number of students (55%) did not feel connected to any adult in the school. When asked what would help them do better in school, students overwhelmingly identified trusting, positive relationships. This finding is supported by the research of Lewin and Regine (2000), which suggests that, when individuals feel connected to an organization, they also feel a deeper sense of purpose.

To enhance communication and relationship-building skills, we must first recognize the value of committing time and energy to this area. Teachers who understand the importance of relationships will engage their students on the first day of class by welcoming them into the class, learning their names as quickly as possible, and gathering information about them. Such teachers are committed to meeting not only students' academic needs, but also their social and emotional needs.

Engagement begins the moment you make eye contact the first time you meet a student. It is important to note, however, that engagement is not a one-time event. As a general rule, we need to engage early and often, keeping in mind that different students will be engaged in different ways. The process of building and sustaining strong, meaningful relationships starts with the understanding that there is potential for good—and even great—things in every person.

Without establishing positive relationships with our students, we will merely be the delivery system for curriculum.

Sylvia's experience with the graffiti artists at her school is a good example. Prior to the mural project, these students were receiving plenty of negative recognition. Sylvia's goal became turning this pattern into positive recognition. Using recognition and engagement to build a relationship based on trust, Sylvia was careful to follow through with her promises to Tao and the other taggers. She knew that once she developed positive, trusting relationships, the taggers would begin to take ownership of the institution. The mural project allowed them to feel personally invested in the school and instilled in them a sense of pride that spilled over into other areas of the school community. These young men had now started to become citizens in the school rather than tourists.

Efforts like this can begin to personalize your school. Students who are engaged and invested in the school and who feel a personal connection to at least one adult can completely shift the climate of the school. Likewise, when students are disengaged, the culture and climate of the school suffers. It is important to keep in mind that personalization must be cultivated every day throughout the organization. The process intensifies when more and more members of the organization see the value of creating and maintaining a personalized environment.

Personalization affects student performance in countless positive ways, and increases the capacity of young people to learn (Hilliard, 2002). When students feel connected to at least one adult at school, they are usually willing to work harder for that individual. Examine your own school experiences. Think back to teachers you had in school. Each of us can immediately recall those teachers who had a positive or negative effect on us. Teachers with whom we had a personalized relationship inspired us to work harder. Probably some of our best grades were earned in classes led by those teachers. What made the difference? It was the relationship between the student and the teacher.

BUILDING RELATIONSHIPS WITH DIFFICULT STAFF

In any change initiative, the greatest roadblock often comes from individuals who undermine the positive efforts of a group. By this we don't mean individuals who question, debate, and even argue tough issues or who present different opinions. In fact, these individuals are helpful to the process. No, the difficult people who act as obstacles to change are those who choose not to participate in the discussion or who attempt to drag others down.

In any organization there are three groups of people: those who are willing to fully participate in the process and work for the betterment of the organization; resisters who want to undermine the change initiative; and those who fall in the middle, who have not decided which group they will align with. Motivating and engaging this middle group so that they take ownership is crucial to the success of any change initiative.

Even if the leader succeeds in influencing the middle group, however, there will still be a percentage of individuals who resist change. It is important to look beyond the resistance and see what the underlying issues are. There may have been events that occurred in their past professional and/or personal lives that are causing the negativity, such as a previous supervisor who they feel did not treat them fairly, or a divorce or illness in the family. Although boundaries are important when it comes to the personal lives of others, if we can help them deal with circumstances that affect their work, we may see a change of attitude.

Faye was a good principal who was having trouble with Judy, a teacher who resisted every school reform effort. One morning while checking the staff absentee list, Faye saw Judy's name; the reason for her absence was listed as "death in family." Checking with her department head, Faye learned that Judy's elderly mother had passed away. Faye wrote a card to Judy offering her condolences, and she called Judy's home that evening and left a message on the answering machine telling her not to worry about her students and classes—Faye and the other teachers would take care of everything. Two days later, Faye made a point of attending the wake for Judy's mother. As Faye reached Judy in the receiving line, Judy was clearly surprised but pleased to see her there.

Early the following week, when Judy returned to school, she came to Faye's office and told her how much it meant to her that Faye had taken time out of her busy schedule to attend the wake. Faye responded that she wanted to offer any support she could and would continue to support her as she went through the adjustment of the loss of a parent.

As Faye reflected on her experiences with Judy in the past, it was clear that Judy had been feeling the effects of her mother's long-term illness. Being a very private person, Judy had shared little of her personal life.

As time went on, Judy's attitude toward school, her students, and Faye improved dramatically. She became more willing to play an active and positive role in school reform efforts. Maybe the change was a result of the reduced stress after coming to terms with her mother's death; maybe it was the kindness Faye extended to her during this difficult time in her life; maybe it was a combination of the two. In any case, the events with Judy reinforced to Faye the power of the personal touch. Acts of kindness can go far when building a foundation of understanding and trust.

BUILDING RELATIONSHIPS WITH DIFFICULT STUDENTS

In any relationship, there are three possible outcomes:

- The relationship is improved.
- The relationship remains unchanged.
- The relationship is damaged.

In adult/student relationships, the three options certainly apply. The difference between adult/student relationships and adult/adult or student/student relationships is that educators have more control in determining the outcome of adult/student relationships. Youth are impulsive by nature. They often act or speak without giving much thought to consequences. As mature adults, we have usually developed a sense of perspective and greater patience that allows us to look at the world through a different lens. In theory, these experiences help us guide youth through the trials and tribulations of adolescence.

By forging relationships with students prior to a confrontational situation, we build a foundation that can help withstand confrontations.

In school, as in life, there are countless teachable moments: the exact moment when the student is mentally and emotionally prepared to receive and process information. A teacher with good communication skills and strong relationships with students knows his or her students well enough to capture and capitalize on these teachable moments.

Consider the case of Joseph, who began to disengage from his school friends and his school work at the end of his sophomore year. He managed to pass all his courses, but did not finish the school year well. Joseph got up every morning at 5:00 a.m. to go to hockey practice; he spent the rest of his free time reading *Car and Driver* magazine. Although Joseph was not doing well in school, he did have interests. A teenager who is willing to get up at 5:00 in the morning to go to a cold hockey rink has a passion. Also, regardless of what he was reading, he *was* reading. For Joseph, there was a lot to build on to reengage him in school and in learning.

At the start of his junior year, it was crucial for Joseph's teachers to build positive relationships with him, identify his interests, and help him reconnect to school. One of Joseph's teachers did an interest inventory the first week of school. On the interest inventory, Joseph noted his interest in hockey and cars—this was just the information the teacher needed to engage Joseph in conversation and craft assignments for Joseph that were linked to his interests. Joseph began to feel more comfortable with his teacher and, in turn, became more engaged in class. The foundation of the relationship had formed and, as his teacher became more interested in Joseph, Joseph became more interested in the class. Without the teacher building a relationship with this young man, there was a very real possibility that he would have never realized his academic potential.

For every educator who sees a new set of learners each semester, the three options apply. The opportunity to improve the relationship, maintain the relationship, or damage the relationship is always at hand. Sometimes it may be a case of three steps forward, two steps back. But by forging the relationship prior to a confrontational situation, we build a foundation that can help withstand such confrontations.

Sometimes that is not possible, and the first encounter with the student is negative. At this point, the actions we as the adults take will determine the future direction of the relationship. This may not be easy. The adults may be hesitant to attempt to re-engage the student, since this attempt may initially be met with a hostile response. However, it is our responsibility to work for a positive outcome. Taking a few proactive steps can minimize the likelihood that the relationship will remain negative:

1. Allow time for the student to calm down.
2. Reengage the student on neutral ground without an audience.
3. Be calm and patient.
4. Speak *with* the student, not *at* the student.
5. Find common ground.
6. Admit the first encounter did not go well—don't blame.
7. LISTEN without interrupting.
8. Stay positive and focused on a better relationship in the future.
9. Immediately reward positive student behaviors.

Strong emotions manifest themselves differently in each person. Younger students have not learned how to keep certain feelings in check and allow these strong feelings to guide behavior that is often inappropriate. Adults often encounter a student for the first time when the student is angry or hurt or even embarrassed by a situation. The nine-step process presented above is an effective way to have a new start with anyone where the first encounter was strained by emotion. It also reaffirms relationship building as an active process that should be embedded in all interactions with students.

Next Steps: Action and Reflection to Build Effective Communication and Relationships

All successful relationships are based on communication and relationships but, often, too little attention is paid to how they "work" in a positive or negative way on a day-to-day basis. Use the following Problem-Based Learning (PBL) exercises to support opportunities for personal and organizational growth related to these two critical elements of Pillar One:

1. Pat the principal is all business, placing an emphasis on efficiency, rules, and order. While most teachers understand and appreciate Pat's efficiency, many feel that their principal is distant and difficult to approach. Some even feel that Pat is aloof and unfriendly. Why do the teachers feel the way they do? What advice would you give to improve Pat's effectiveness with the faculty?

2. Andre is an administrator who always asks employees "How are you?" at the beginning of every conversation. Some people feel that Andre doesn't listen to their responses, and others view him as insincere. What behaviors might be negatively impacting Andre's effectiveness? What behaviors would assure his employees that Andre is listening?

3. Take a personal inventory of your communication skill set. Consider the following questions:

(a) How well do I share my ideas of where I think this school should be heading? Rate yourself on a scale of 1-10, with 10 being the very best communicator.

(b) Do you communicate best in the verbal form or the written form?

(c) When communicating with others, do you consider all those who need to know and others who would like to know about initiatives? List two stakeholder groups that you most often overlook.

(d) "Empathic listening" requires that you listen to another's feelings "using your eyes." What do you think is meant by this statement?

4. Identify an element of your school's operations that could use improvement. As a first step, ask those closest to it to be part of a small problem-solving team to study the issue and develop possible solutions. Part of your job will be to encourage the development of communications skills among the members of the group. So model your best communication skills and lend plenty of personal support to the team as they work. Empower the team to implement change after an agreed-upon strategy emerges.

CHAPTER TWO

PILLAR TWO:
LEADERSHIP AND
EMPOWERMENT

"Leaders are visionaries with a poorly developed sense of fear,
and no concept of the odds against them."
—Robert Jarvick

Throughout history, countless leaders have changed our world for good or bad. These leaders exist at all levels in every society and organization, and schools are no exception. We see examples of leadership throughout the school community. These people may be teachers, administrators, support staff, students, or students' family members. Who they are isn't as important as what they do: Leaders have the power to change organizations for the better.

Good leaders can and do make a difference in schools. Lorraine Monroe (1997) wrote this story of courageous leadership in New York City in her book *Nothing's Impossible:*

If you've heard of me, it's probably because of the Frederick Douglas Academy, a special high school in New York's Harlem that I had the privilege of helping to found and run. The academy's success in teaching inner-city kids has won it a lot of attention, including a profile on TV's *60 Minutes*—one of our society's "official" marks of recognition.

As I write these words, in the spring of 1997, the academy is about to graduate its first class of twelfth-graders. About three-quarters of the seniors have already received letters of acceptance to college, and our counselors expect nearly all the rest to be accepted, too. Most of the students haven't yet decided which schools they'll attend, but their acceptances have come from many colleges, including Columbia, Dartmouth, NYU, and the University of Pennsylvania to Temple, Spellman, Morehouse, Colgate, and Smith. (p. 1)

Dr. Monroe goes on to tell the story of how she transformed a public high school in a large urban area into a beacon of hope to the 80% African American and 20% Latino students it serves. While the statistics of low socioeconomic status and children from broken homes plays out for the students and their families who go to the Frederick Douglas Academy, as they do in many urban settings across this country, the transformation from a failing school to a center of educational excellence is possible anywhere. Leadership is what makes the difference.

Leaders have the power to change organizations for the better.

This chapter will discuss the qualities that make a true leader such as Lorraine Monroe. Four of these qualities are courageous vision informed by an attitude of caring and compassion, the ability to face reality (and to make sure others do too), the ability to empower others, and the willingness to adapt to change.

THE COURAGEOUS, VISIONARY LEADER

We have all witnessed the changes that can occur with the addition or absence of particular faculty, school staff, or students. A new department head may turn around the department; a new head custodian may foster pride in the interior and exterior of the building; a new student council president may mobilize the student body into positive action. Each of these leaders can have a dramatic positive impact on a school if he or she is the right person in the right position.

What quality enables the leader to accomplish things with purpose and focus? Leaders who have a clear and compelling vision are able to achieve initiatives with purpose and focus; purpose and vision are intrinsically linked. In our view, the best leaders have what we call a *leadership mindset,* which combines courageous vision with a selfless, caring manner. Kouzes and Posner (2006) wrote:

> When we move on, people do not remember us for what we do for ourselves. They remember us for what we do for them. One of the great joys and grave responsibilities of leaders is making sure that those in their care live lives not only of success but also of significance. (p. 10)

Having a purpose that is not centered on "what's in it for me" gives a leader the ability to set the stage for taking risks for the right reasons. The visionary leader shares a view of how to do things better and gives those within the organization the freedom to take risks without fear of reprimand. He or she provides followers with a glimpse of how good we could make things when we all have the courage to do our work in a caring, selfless manner and continually help others succeed.

According to Robert Jarvick, inventor of the first artificial heart, leaders are visionaries. His quote at the beginning of this chapter implies that leaders are individuals who imagine what could be. They cannot be stifled or intimidated; they are focused on where they want to go and will not be negatively influenced by others. For them, the impossible is just another degree of difficulty, another challenge to overcome.

The best leaders have what we call a leadership mindset, which combines courageous vision with a selfless, caring manner.

THE ABILITY TO DEAL IN REALITY

"I never did give anybody hell. I just told them the truth and they thought it was hell." This famous quote by President Harry S. Truman exemplifies a second characteristic of leadership: the ability to deal in reality.

In *Good to Great: Why Some Companies Make the Leap...And Others Don't,* Collins calls dealing in reality "confronting the brutal facts" (2001, p. 65). Bossidy, Charan, and Burck (2002) point out that successful corporations are those that face and deal in reality. Change efforts based on inaccurate information are ultimately likely to collapse. The same applies to schools. It's crucial to know where you are organizationally in respect to both internal and external factors.

Too often, individuals in leadership positions paint a picture of a situation or organization that is unrealistically positive. Dealing in reality is one of the top responsibilities of a true leader. By dealing honestly with issues, effective leaders gain the trust and confidence of others. Juan, the new principal of a large urban high school, is a good example.

Juan replaced a principal who had held the position for nearly 18 years. Over that time, the community had changed and the school's academics and climate had declined. The daily school routine was plagued with gang graffiti, handshakes, and colors. Staff and students were primarily concerned with safety, rather than education. As a result, academics suffered tremendously: SAT and other standardized test scores were at an all-time low. Enrollment in honors courses had declined and student failure rates had increased, especially among ninth-grade students. The high teen pregnancy rate became a chronic problem. The school was plagued with increases in the dropout rate, as well as high student and staff absenteeism.

When Juan began to research how stakeholder groups saw the school, he found most folks clinging to the past and focusing on a time when conditions were better. People had not yet accepted the changes facing the school and community; they were just hoping that things would improve, even though there was no concrete plan for making this happen—a dangerous game to play. Leaders who operate with this mentality may create negative conditions that will take years to overcome.

Juan felt the strained academic culture and climate of the school most sharply only a few days into his new leadership position. While walking the halls, he noticed a feature film being shown in one classroom. When he asked the teacher to explain the relationship of the film to her curriculum, she explained that it did not relate—it was simply a reward the students could earn every week for "being good." Astoundingly, the teacher added that, because Juan was new, he did not understand that this was not an academic school—the staff's priority was to keep the students quiet and happy. After that conversation, it was clear to Juan that there could be no band-aid approach; the school was in need of major surgery.

The administration that preceded Juan had fostered a culture that was not dealing in reality. Instead of looking at the big picture or heeding the warning signs, the school was operating from day to day. Had the school leadership recognized and faced the changes that were taking place within the community, it could have taken a proactive approach to meeting the needs of both students and staff. The ability to closely examine and monitor the external environment and to adapt accordingly is an important quality of any effective leader.

Juan knew that he needed to get the faculty and staff to deal in reality. At a faculty meeting, Juan passed out a 3″x5″ card to each of the 300-plus faculty and staff members. He asked them each to write what they perceived to be the three most positive aspects of the school on one side of the card and their perceptions of the school's three greatest challenges on the other side.

After completing the activity, Juan collected all the cards and culled out common themes. The faculty and staff had consistently noted that one of the most positive aspects of the school was the faculty and staff. It was clear they felt they were an exceptional group of educators. The primary response for the three greatest challenges was the students. Armed with this information, Juan held another meeting and shared the results with the faculty and staff. He did not share with the group his reaction to the information but, rather, he asked the faculty and staff to examine the information and explain their analysis of the data. Divided into groups of eight, staff members examined the results of the 3″x5″ card activity.

At times the table discussions were heated. It was clear that individuals had strong opinions of the information collected. As Juan pulled the groups back together to share their analyses, the groups began to realize that they were laying blame on students, parents, and administration—there was clearly an external locus of control. As the discussions continued, more and more staff members began to realize that they held some responsibility for the conditions at the school.

This was a breakthrough moment for Juan and he seized it. He began talking to the faculty and staff about what they had control over, what they could influence, and what was beyond their control. The discussions continued at subsequent meetings, and ownership for the challenges began to shift. The faculty and staff began to adopt an internal locus of control. The shift had begun to take place, and the faculty and staff began to feel empowered to make changes that impacted student achievement and the culture of the school.

This transformation took time and there were still resisters but more and more of the faculty and staff believed that they could make a difference; it was the beginning of a total transformation of the school.

The Ability to Empower Others

For Juan's school, the external environment included the high-stakes testing mandated at the state level. The current environment of accountability has affected schools in every state, and proactive school leaders have faced the opportunities and challenges it has posed. Juan knew his task was to help the faculty, students, and parents understand the importance and value of high-stakes assessments. But he did not make any unilateral decisions about how to solve this problem. Instead, he shared his vision of a return to high performance through a collaborative effort. With the help of a nucleus of leaders from multiple stakeholder groups, Juan was able to build the state standards-based testing into a new strategic plan for the school. The key to accomplishing this was fostering ownership at all levels.

He began with the school's academic and standards committee, empowering it to make his vision operational. Juan gave the academic and standards committee the authority to make the decisions necessary to raise academic achievement. He did not tell them how to do it, but he shared with them that he had the confidence and trust in them that they could make decisions for the school. The committee selected the state standards-based assessment as one of two critical areas for academic improvement and designed an action plan that focused on improving student scores. An important piece of this effort was developing marketing strategies to demonstrate the importance and value of this type of assessment to all stakeholders, including students and parents.

Juan's example of empowering others and making sure that success was celebrated and shared helped stakeholders buy in to the goal of a better life. The cultural shift began with this first success. Like the small, fragile sprout on the seed that is nurtured to become a beautiful, mighty oak tree, cultural change can be made sustainable and strong over time with the right plan.

Rather than learning from events that take place in other schools or communities, ineffective leaders are content to maintain the status quo.

Willingness to Adapt

Successful school leaders understand that the school's skill set may need to change to meet changing conditions of the external environment. These conditions can come from beyond the local community. Events at state, regional, national, and even international levels can affect what a school's skill set needs to be. For example, from a school safety perspective, the events of September 11, 2001 changed the way all schools viewed the potential for a terrorist attack in their area. Since that event, proactive school leaders have factored plans for dealing with crisis situations into their school's safety equation, reviewing the safety and security procedures in place and working with others to identify gaps.

Ineffective leaders, however, only feel a sense of relief that their school was not directly affected by a tragedy. The tendency for this type of leader is to think, "It couldn't happen here," or "Someone else in the district is responsible for taking care of such procedures." Rather than learning from events that take place in other schools or communities, ineffective leaders are content to maintain the status quo. Thus, in a serious situation, they are more likely to be reactive rather than proactive.

Janet was an elementary school principal in a community that had traditionally been comprised of middle-class families who had lived in the community for generations. As companies in the community began to move their operations to other parts of the country, the demographics of the community began to change.

Families that had lived in the community for generations began to move, and the neighborhoods around the school became more transient. More homes were being rented, and students and parents were less invested in the neighborhoods and the school. The elementary school was getting a new kind of student. The faculty and administration were going to have to learn new skills to adapt to the changing dynamics of the student and parent population.

Seeing the shift, Janet pulled the faculty together and began sharing her observations of the changes that were taking place. She shared relevant data with the faculty regarding student mobility rates, shifts in housing from home ownership to rental properties, and data relating to student performance and academic needs. In turn, Janet asked the faculty for their observations: what they were seeing in their classrooms, with their students, and with parents with whom they had interacted. Janet noted that the faculty's assessment of the changes were consistent with hers.

The school's skill set was going to need to change based on the changes in the community. Janet and her leadership team mobilized community agencies to provide additional social services within the school. They had focus group meetings in the community in the evenings to reach out to parents, share information about the school, and dialogue with parents about their needs. This kind of outreach went a long way in building trust with families and children.

Janet saw the changes that were taking place in the community and realized that the school needed to adapt to these changing conditions. She took a proactive approach and worked with the faculty, community, parents, and children to better meet their needs. Although it is impossible to prepare for every scenario, a leader who anticipates potential influences from both internal and external sources will surely be better prepared as changes occur.

Next Steps: Action and Reflection to Develop Leadership and a Sense of Empowerment in Members of the School Community

There are two facets of life worth getting right. The warmth of a family where one feels loved and safe to be one's self is one facet; the other is a healthy work environment in which people feel appreciated and are willing to take risks. It would be great if we all went to work the way the seven dwarfs did in the Walt Disney animated film "Snow White and the Seven Dwarfs"—high-stepping, whistling, and singing. As a leader who empowers others, it is your job to bring that kind of feeling to everyone who comes to work. A higher quality of life within the organization results in higher-quality output from those who do the work. Use the following PBL exercises to support opportunities for personal and organizational growth that can enhance leadership and create a sense of empowerment across the organization:

1. A new principal inherits a school that has been run by a "grouch" for the last 15 years. The faculty works hard but never laughs; everything is taken seriously. Fun is not to be found at faculty meetings. Is it important to make a working environment pleasant and sometimes fun? Why or why not? What advice would you give the new principal for meetings and day-to-day interactions?

2. Principal Terry constantly looks for ways to empower the faculty and student body. Terry knows that those

closest to the problem are the most likely to develop the best solutions. Terry also knows that trust is a powerful motivator for employees and students. List two specific responsibilities that are typically handled by the administration that could be managed successfully by each of the following groups:

(a) Teachers
(b) Students
(c) Support staff

3. Organize PBL teams by skill and interest sets (differences can work in these cases), and allow them to solve real problems of the organization. For example, bring together a group of school staff members and ask them to collaborate on developing a dream of your school as a perfect place to work. This dream can require both small and big changes, some that cost nothing and others that would be costly to implement. Work with the group to identify "possible now" elements and have them act as partners with you in moving the plan forward. Remember that the first step should take into account Pillar One—the work group should *communicate* its dream to the rest of the staff and ask for reactions and ideas. While resources may act as a barrier to implementing all the suggestions, encourage the group to hold onto its vision and to continue looking for ways to move the school toward it, even with limited resources.

CHAPTER THREE

PILLAR THREE: PLANNING AND EVALUATION

"Beliefs don't always match facts."
– Steven Edwards

It has been said that failure to plan is planning to fail. With that in mind, effective planning focuses on four fundamental questions:

- Where are we now?
- Where do we want to be?
- How will we get there?
- How will we know when we are there?

Good planning is impossible without good data collection and analysis to answer the first question. Answering the other three questions—*Where do we want to be? How do we get there?* and *How will we know when we are there?*—begins with knowing where we are **now**. For that reason, this chapter includes an extensive case study illustrating the principles of effective collection of data for planning, evaluation, and decision making. It also discusses the process of turning data into a sustainable improvement plan, and provides an example of what can happen when planning is flawed.

COLLECTING, ANALYZING, AND USING DATA: A CASE STUDY

Sandra was a principal of a large suburban high school of 2,400 students where fighting had become an issue. Sandra's days were consumed with running from fight to fight. Countless times throughout the school day she would hear "code 14" on her walkie-talkie, which meant a fight was in progress.

Because gangs and gang activity were prevalent at the school, Sandra and her leadership team assumed that the majority of fights were gang-related. If this assumption was true, Sandra and her colleagues would need to design appropriate strategies to reduce the gang-related fights. But without a closer look, how could the leadership team be sure? Sandra was savvy enough to know that what seemed logical to her and her leadership team members needed to be confirmed or disproved through accurate data collection and analysis.

Data Collection: Where Are We Now?

Before Sandra and the team began to collect data, they considered a number of key points. First, they needed to define the problem. What did they mean by student fighting? For the leadership team's purposes, they defined fighting as an incident between two or more individuals where there was unwanted physical contact. Defining the problem in context is essential before data collection can begin.

Second, Sandra and her team needed to consider what kinds of data to collect. It is often advisable to collect both quantitative and qualitative data to find answers to problems of interest. Quantitative data relies purely on numbers and gives a wider view of the issue. Qualitative data focuses on an up-close view and is often based on observations and interviews. Using both types of data ensures that the issue is being examined on multiple levels and from a variety of perspectives.

The school created a standardized format for collecting and reporting data on fighting incidents, which included the day of the week, the time of day, the location, and the grade level, gender, and race of the participants. In addition, the team conducted student interviews, read incident reports, and questioned participants and witnesses extensively. All school faculty and staff were trained on how to collect and report data. Sandra and the leadership team were careful to collect only data that was relevant to the topic, and they made certain that the data collection was consistent over time. To know where they wanted to go, Sandra first had to determine where they were. The data analysis allowed them to answer that question and enabled them to establish a plan as to where they wanted to go. Using the data, Sandra and the team set a target, a percentage they wanted to achieve in the reduction of the number of fights they were having.

Teams often focus on the goal of where they want to go without determining where they really are. It is difficult—if not impossible—to reach point B if you don't know where point A (your starting point) is. Once Sandra and her team determined where they were (by collecting and analyzing the data on fighting incidents in the school) and where they wanted to go (a specific percentage reduction in the number of fights), they could answer the second question—*"How do you know when you get there?"*—by continuing to track data in order to assess progress, modify their plan as new information became available, and reflect on their practices to set new targets.

Another important data collection strategy the team used was to collect data from multiple sources. For instance, the in-school security team kept incident reports on all altercations, and the three assistant principals kept a record of all fights and disputes. Also, the school resource officers (SROs) kept data on incidents of fighting that involved an arrest. The leadership team also found teacher input and information to be an invaluable source of data.

Since multiple sources of data were collected, members of each of these data-collecting groups would meet weekly to examine data and identify any conflicting reports or common themes. Bringing multiple stakeholders together to analyze data and make recommendations based on that data leads to building a collaborative culture and ownership at multiple levels within the organization.

Along with examining internal data on incidents of fighting, Sandra's team also made use of community data. The SROs were instrumental in providing crime and violence statistics from the community. Tracking similar types of incidents in the community allowed them to draw comparisons between school and community data, and thus possibly forecast trends.

Making quick judgments based on limited data only contributes to poor decision making. In addition to looking for trends, data should be disaggregated to identify patterns within particular populations, such as grade level, gender, and race. Those closest to the problem—in the case of Sandra's school, school administrators, security officers, teachers, SROs, and the school leadership team—should be involved in asking the question: "What do these data tell us?"

Bringing multiple stakeholders together to analyze data and make recommendations based on that data leads to building a collaborative culture and ownership at multiple levels within the organization.

At Sandra's school, the leadership team's collection and analysis of quantitative data on school fighting yielded some interesting results. First, they found that fighting was most likely to occur on Mondays during the month of March. The majority of incidents took place during the 5-minute student passing time after lunch and prior to the beginning of the last period of the day. Sandra's team also found that the majority of altercations took place at or very close to exit six, an area where students were funneled into a large lobby from the gymnasium, the student cafeteria, the second floor, and two additional major hallways.

Disaggregating the data by grade level, gender, and race, the leadership team found that the highest incidence of fighting occurred among ninth-graders. This did not surprise anyone, as previous data indicated that academic and behavioral problems peaked in ninth grade. The numbers also clearly demonstrated a disproportionate number of female students engaging in aggressive behavior. Further analysis by race showed that a disproportionate number of fights were among African American students.

Collecting qualitative data proved to be just as valuable in understanding the problem. Information from interviews, eyewitness accounts, and incident descriptions helped determine that the causes of the fights most often centered on boyfriend/girlfriend arguments and issues. Furthermore, "he said/she said" rumors initiated by third parties who were feeding information to both potential combatants often sparked fights. Taken together, the team's quantitative and qualitative data analysis gave a concrete, comprehensive set of facts that the school could use to begin addressing the fighting problem.

How Do We Get There? Part 1: Identifying Needs

Once the information was gathered, how could it be used to make positive changes? The first realization Sandra and her leadership team made was that they had been wrong about why fights were occurring. Rather than being gang-related, most altercations were sparked by relationship issues among ninth-grade African American girls.

The leadership team identified 20 girls who were repeatedly involved in the fights, and Sandra scheduled an informal group meeting with them to discuss this issue. After welcoming the group and offering refreshments, Sandra introduced the problem—that each student in the room had been involved in frequent altercations—and explained how these incidents were harming everyone. For example, countless hours of education had already been lost through the students' collective suspensions. Many of them had suffered personal injury or had caused injury to other students and staff; some of the students had even been arrested. Teachers and administrators had spent many hours dealing with these incidents—hours that could have been spent on instruction and other educational opportunities.

Sandra indicated to the group that continued fighting would lead to more significant disciplinary action, even expulsion from school. The focus of this meeting, she said, was to avoid that. She wanted to work *with* the young ladies—not against them—to develop a solution.

At first, the girls' responses focused on blame; they pointed fingers at others and were not willing to accept responsibility for their actions. Sandra gently insisted that the girls focus on solutions—How could they collectively reduce the incidents of fighting among the group? Finally, one student spoke up: "There's nothing to do around here." Sandra expressed surprise. The school offered a wide range of clubs, athletic teams, and activity programs. But, clearly, she had missed their point. Another student declared, "We want step." Naively, Sandra asked what step was. Shocked that she did not know, the girls rose to their feet and began stomping their feet and slapping their hands in rhythm. "That's step!" they said. Realizing that this was an opportunity she needed to seize, Sandra promised the girls that, if they stopped fighting, she would ensure the implementation of a school step team.

How Do We Get There? Part 2: Implementing Data-Driven Solutions

True to her word, Sandra set out to establish a step team for the girls. Within a few weeks, they had a step team of 40 members, which began performing during halftime at basketball games. In fact, the group became so popular that it was invited to perform at regional events throughout the state and, eventually, at conferences and programs across the country.

Had Sandra and her leadership team not been data-driven, they may never have started a step team. Data collection and analysis over a reasonable period of time enabled them to clearly identify problems and then develop solutions. Data collection also allowed them to separate perception from reality.

Starting the step team did not eliminate all fighting, but it did significantly reduce the number of incidents. In addition, it helped Sandra to realize that she needed to devote more attention to the students' needs and become a better listener. The challenge was to meet the diverse needs of the students in her school, and a solution was to use data collection and analysis to help drive the school in that direction.

Beyond starting the step team, Sandra and her team also used the data to change traffic patterns and increase adult supervision in the area where students exited the cafeteria, the location pinpointed as the site of most fights. All students had been leaving the cafeteria on the west side and then walking through the gymnasium lobby and doorway by exit six instead of using other exits on the east side of the cafeteria. The leadership team decided to split the tables in the cafeteria into two groups. The students seated on the east side would now exit through the east side doors; the other half would exit through the west side doors. This simple change significantly reduced the number of students dumping into exit six, which in turn contributed to an overall reduction in fighting incidents.

By looking critically at data, school leaders can build a strong foundation that will create the opportunity for results-oriented planning.

Because the data also indicated that March was a particularly bad month for incidents of fighting, the students and staff collaborated to create a "March Madness" program. Activities included a three-on-three basketball tournament held after school and makeovers sponsored by local salons. A big hit was the free donut cart managed by the assistant principals and Sandra. At the beginning of first period, Sandra would stop at classrooms and ask the teacher whether 95% of the class was in attendance, if all students had arrived on time, and if 90% of all homework had been completed. If the answers to all three questions were yes, the students would each receive a donut and juice.

March Madness also rewarded the class (freshmen, sophomores, juniors, or seniors) that maintained the lowest percentage of behavioral incidents with an assembly activity at the end of the month. These assemblies also created relevant learning experiences for students, as they generally included speakers from cultural centers within the community or from the local university. Often students' talents would be showcased during the assemblies, and school leaders realized that giving students the opportunity to perform in front of their classmates and teachers deepened their engagement with the school.

Sandra and the leadership team also posted information in the cafeteria and library media center highlighting the effects of violence on individuals and society. Finally, they used morning announcements to provide continual positive reminders on proper conduct in and around school. During the first year of the March Madness program, the combined efforts resulted in a 32% drop in incidents of fighting for the month.

The initial success of the March Madness program extended over a 10-year period, in which incidents of fighting dropped by almost two-thirds. Sandra and the leadership team were able to accomplish this because of their effective use of data. They identified and defined the problem, developed a hypothesis about the causes of the problem, and used data collection and analysis to test the hypothesis. They were then able to develop a number of interventions to address the problem. Their tracking system enabled them to determine on a continuing basis whether they had gotten to where they wanted to be—a school where fighting was rare and students felt safe and engaged.

As educators continue to be held to higher levels of accountability, the effective collection and analysis of data is particularly valuable. We must abandon practices of basing decisions on perception rather than reality—of seeking the quick fix and never addressing the real issue. By looking critically at data, school leaders can build a strong foundation that will create the opportunity for results-oriented planning.

FROM DATA TO RESULTS: OWNING THE PLAN

How many times have you heard, "We've done this before"? Every educator has participated in a planning process at least once; most of us have done so numerous times. In many cases, that process has fallen short of achieving its intended goals. Although a fancy report with a beautiful cover may have been generated, the plan was never taken to the implementation phase. Not surprisingly, individuals who have experienced this process are reluctant to go through it again—and, even if forced to do so, they are unlikely to take ownership of the plan.

Yet there *are* schools across the nation where both data and an effective planning process have been used to achieve measurable and documented results. What have these schools done different-ly? Five key elements separate schools that have achieved notable results from those that have just gone through the motions: They deal in reality, develop a plan, create ownership of the plan, em-power others by establishing leadership at all levels, and stick to the process.

Sharing the Data

After you collect data, it is crucial to share it with all stakeholders—faculty and staff, central office administration, students, parents, and the community at large—and carefully explain it. If anything is left to misinterpretation, the results may be catastrophic. For example, the data Sandra and her leadership team collected on fighting could have been interpreted in several negative ways (e.g., people may have focused on the high number of fights or the specific ethnic groups involved and the administration may have been pressured into quick fixes, such as more suspensions and expulsions). Careful explanation of the data is critical to presenting a concrete action plan for how you will address the problems identified by the data.

Organizing for Planning

After presenting the data to stakeholder groups, the next step is to recruit volunteers who are willing to participate in an action planning process. These volunteers should come from a wide range of stakeholder groups, sometimes including the board of education members and central office, as well as those who are part of the school community. From this core group, a strong facilitator can usually be found. Planning should be strategic and also focus on identifying key strategies to address needs in four central areas:

- Academics and standards
- School climate and student behavior
- Facilities, equipment, and technology
- Community and community resources

Any strategic planning endeavor should focus on school improvement in each of these interconnected areas. Planning should address not only specific problems, but also assets and strengths.

Success for a strategic plan hinges on an open and honest relationship between the facilitator and site leaders—what Covey (1989) calls *synergy*:

> Synergy is the essence of principle-centered leadership.... It catalyzes, unites, and unleashes the greatest powers within people....What is synergy? Simply defined, it means that the whole is greater than the sum of its parts. (pp. 262-283)

 Without synergy between the facilitator and the principal (the two individuals who will serve as the catalyst for change), any initiative is headed for failure or, at best, minimal results.

Selecting a Planning Tool

Planning tools can be helpful in guiding the process. The planning model you select needs to reflect the unique talents and abilities of the planning team; their economic, gender, and age differences; and their range of educational backgrounds and experiences. One effective model, the *Social Reconnaissance Model*, was developed during World War II by the military. It has been revised numerous times and adapted to serve as an effective planning tool in a variety of settings. It can help teams move from problem identification to action planning in a relatively easy and efficient manner. In addition, the model works well when your goal is to build

consensus among a group of people who come from diverse social, cultural, and educational backgrounds. More information
on this model can be found at http://www.cchd.us/links/social_
reconnaissance_community_discussion_group_process.pdf.

After selecting the model, the next step is to select and train team
leaders to lead planning in each of the four school improvement
areas. An advantage of the *Social Reconnaissance Model* is that the
facilitator and the team leaders do not need to be content experts;
their role is purely facilitation.

The Impact of Poor Planning

Planning needs to be a comprehensive process. When making
decisions about organizational improvement, it is fruitless to use
sound data in one area when you have neglected another. The experience of Public High School illustrates this point.

In the early 1990s, mathematics achievement was below state standards at Public High School and had been continually dropping;
the pressure was on to raise scores. The district's K-12 curriculum
coordinator for mathematics had the responsibility of addressing
falling scores. Part of his plan was to institute integrated mathematics as the curriculum for students in grades 9 and 10.

The idea behind integrated mathematics is the integration of the
key concepts of Algebra I, Geometry, and Algebra II into one
course. From the coordinator's perspective, the plan would provide
students with a better understanding of important mathematical
principles and make clear the connections among three formerly
distinct courses.

The logic made sense and research supported the model, but, unfortunately, there was a flaw. The mathematics coordinator had researched the theories behind integrated mathematics; he had attended workshops and was confident this was the correct approach to help raise student math achievement. The problem was that he had not secured the buy-in of key stakeholders; he had not shared his plan with teachers, parents, or students.

At the end of the school year, teachers were provided with 5 days of professional development; they were given a crash course in integrated mathematics, introduced to the textbook, and instructed to prepare for using integrated mathematics in the fall. There was immediate resistance, which mounted as the summer went on. Word quickly got out to the parents, resulting in an immediate outcry. Parents were expecting their children to take Algebra or Geometry—what was integrated mathematics? They discussed their discomfort about integrated math with their children, causing students to return to school predisposed to resist the change.

Planning needs to be a comprehensive process. When making decisions about organizational improvement, it is fruitless to use sound data in one area when you have neglected another.

Because teachers, parents, and students were against the program, failure was essentially guaranteed. Integrated mathematics may have been an outstanding program, but without buy-in from the key stakeholders during the inception stage, implementation of any initiative is difficult, if not impossible. Parents, teachers, and students applied consistent pressure to revert to the traditional mathematics sequence. After 1 year, integrated mathematics was dropped, and the textbooks were sold to another school district. In this case, the lack of planning cost the school time and money and damaged its effectiveness in preparing young people for the future.

Next Steps: Planning and Evaluation

The shared vision is the foundation for how your group develops its plan and evaluates progress toward its goals. Again, there are four critical questions associated with planning and evaluation:

1. Where are we now?
2. Where do we want to be?
3. How will we get there?
4. How will we know when we get there?

If all stakeholders are looking at the organization as a non-static entity that can either move forward or backward, asking the four critical questions holds a common linkage for organizational growth. Consider the following exercises:

1. Build your own personal goal calendar. Start with short-term goals and extend the calendar to longer-term goals. Use critical question #1 (Where are we now?) to identify your baseline or starting point. Decide what the benchmarks are by applying critical question #2 (Where do we want to be?). Jot down things you will do—creating a calendar of these to-do items—by considering critical question number #3 (How will we get there?). As you reach the benchmark dates, reapply critical question number #1 and, as you move closer to your goal, assess if you have reached it by applying your answers to question #4 (How will we know when we get there?).

2. Share one school improvement effort with which you are familiar that failed from a lack of planning or evaluation. Be honest without being critical. How could this effort have been improved?

3. Evaluate a current school improvement effort in which you are engaged. Has that effort fully answered the four critical questions? What, if anything, needs to occur to address each question?

4. Model the application of Pillar Three, Planning and Evaluation, by using it with all group work you engage in and encourage others to try this approach to achieving individual and group goals.

CHAPTER FOUR

PILLAR FOUR:
COLLABORATION

Coming together is a beginning. Keeping together is a process.
Working together is success.
—Henry Ford

In the mid-1980s, the motion picture "Teachers" was released. The movie highlights one teacher, nicknamed Ditto, whose instructional method consists of distributing mimeographed worksheets that students complete in silence as Ditto reads his newspaper. When Ditto suffers a heart attack and dies during class, the students don't even notice. And since Ditto has always operated in isolation from the rest of the staff, it's some time before anyone else in the school realizes that he has passed away.

Although this Hollywood example takes isolationism to an extreme, the point remains: Throughout our educational history, teachers in this country typically have operated in individual silos, and had little—if any—collaboration with peers. The nature of education creates an environment in which teachers work in isolation, each in his or her own classroom, completely separated from the teacher next door. This problem is exacerbated at the secondary level, where departmentalization creates further isolation.

Organizational growth requires that schools break this traditional approach and become more collaborative—both internally and externally. But effective collaboration does not happen by accident; it requires ongoing communication, strong relationships, and trust. In this chapter, we briefly describe the dangers of isolation and tell the story of Bob, a principal who built internal collaboration by bringing all members of his faculty into the planning process. We then discuss several examples of effective school leaders who achieved a variety of benefits from external collaboration with stakeholders in the community.

Vision may have its beginnings as a leader's solitary thought, but it can only become reality through collaboration.

THE DANGERS OF ISOLATION

Goodlad (1997) warned that education becomes corrupted when stakeholders work in isolation "with everyone competing for their own ends and means" (p. 120). Teaching and learning should be done in the context of collaborative problem solving. Yet in many schools, teachers still work in isolation, receiving minimal feedback on what they are doing—perhaps with just one formal evaluation by the school principal every 3 years.

Countless schools across the country foster this sense of isolation, either within their building or between their building and other schools in the district. Many district elementary, middle, and high schools operate independently, and in some cases, even in competition with one another based on the comparison of their scores on high-stakes tests. In cases like this, the real or perceived pressure to excel forces schools into an "us versus them" mentality that, in the long run, is counterproductive to student achievement and success. Goodlad's warning foretells what comes of this practice: "Everyone loses" (p. 120).

Not only do schools traditionally work in isolation from one another, but they often also operate in isolation from their communities. When this happens, valuable resources from the external environment are untapped, leaving schools to rely only on the talents and resources available within their walls.

Once we understand the possible negative effects of isolation, we also realize that the value of collaboration at every level cannot be overstated. Success in the long term will not be measured by individual accomplishments, but rather by collaborative efforts.

BUILDING A TEAM

Bob was the energetic principal of a large urban middle school of 1,000 students. After being on the job for 1 year, he concluded that the only way he and the faculty would be able to achieve success, as measured by the students' social, emotional, and academic achievement, was to bring the talents of many together.

Bob knew that safety was a major concern of staff members. Teachers had retreated to the sanctuary of their own classrooms, where they perceived a greater sense of security and control. This trend among the teachers only increased the isolation within the school; rather than making them safer, it actually made them more vulnerable.

When teachers operate in isolation, depersonalization occurs, affecting the school's climate on all fronts and jeopardizing the social, emotional, and academic well-being of the institution. Turning this around requires creative problem solving through collaboration among all internal and external stakeholders.

In our discussion of the planning process, we noted the need for collaboration and ownership for successful implementation of any initiative. Building a culture for collaboration requires that you get people talking to one another. However, this only happens when you create multiple opportunities for staff interaction.

In his first year as principal, Bob observed that such interaction did occur within the school's planning process and decided to use the social reconnaissance model to bring his staff together and create a collaborative culture. However, collaborative opportunities only existed for those who participated. What about those who were not at the table? They were still clinging to an old paradigm. For Bob's school to be successful in its change process, he needed to continually seek out ways to engage multiple stakeholders in the collaborative process and nurture the belief that they were all part of a team.

Involving Internal Stakeholders

To inspire his staff to start thinking of continuous school improvement as a worthwhile goal, Bob asked the faculty to picture how the school would look if everyone came each day with the determination to do a better job than the day before. The discussion sparked by this thought-provoking question resulted in the identification on an important strategy—*all* staff members would participate on individual school improvement teams. School improvement teams included teams devoted to the following areas:

- Curriculum and instruction
- Climate and culture
- Student support services
- Visioning
- Beyond the bell (after-school and summer programs)
- Community partnerships
- Students first (student recognition initiatives)
- Parents and families
- Re-entry (students returning from out-placements/ incarceration)

Each school improvement team was tasked with developing an action plan to address a specific problem identified through data collection and analysis. With the entire staff arranged in action teams, the opportunity for meaningful collaboration increased dramatically.

One reason Bob and his colleagues were successful in the school improvement process was that staff members were allowed to indicate their first-, second-, or third-choice team, and in most cases, they were assigned to their first or second choice. When we give people choices and actively involve them in the process, we increase personal commitment to making the shared vision come true.

However, the leadership team intentionally kept some control of the process. This allowed them to ensure that members from the same department were divided equally among the action teams in order to promote better communication across the school and also prevent cliques within the staff signing up for the same team. While this might seem like micromanaging, it is critical to establish a healthy mix of individuals on each action team; teams composed of friends or cliques are more myopic in their view of the task. When dividing your staff into collaborative groups, the goal should always be maximum diversity in terms of gender, ethnicity, level of experience, teaching assignment (mix departments), level of commitment (divide the resisters among groups), and potential contributions to the group. Careful consideration of team selection will foster greater communication and more meaningful collaboration. The greater the communication and collaboration, the greater the possible net gains.

Bringing the Outside In

After involving internal stakeholders, the next crucial step is engaging external stakeholders. In reality, schools are just a microcosm of the community; whatever exists in the community will exist in the schools. If there is prosperity within the community, there will be prosperity within the school. Likewise, if there is poverty in the community, there will be poverty in the schools. There is no escaping the assets or ills of the school's external environment.

Schools are now being asked to provide more and more services to their students, and although the needs are great, the resources are often scarce. One way to meet the needs of students is through formal and informal partnerships with public and private community agencies and individuals within the community. School leaders should continually extend their outreach to potential community partners.

To meet the needs of the whole child, school leaders must use all the resources available. And when we think we have exhausted those resources, we must look further and challenge our creativity. The following sections highlight some ways to engage stakeholders at a deeper level.

We Can't Teach Them if They're Not in School

Marian was the principal of an urban elementary school that served the poorest district of the city. Absenteeism was a serious problem. One reason for the high absenteeism was student illness; most students lacked adequate medical care and had limited or no insurance coverage.

Marian understood the concept of the full-service school and was certain that added services in or close to the school would improve attendance rates. She shared her vision with some of her faculty members and a few key stakeholders from the community, and they began to seek opportunities that would provide students with additional services.

In cooperation with a local hospital, Marian and her team wrote and applied for a federal grant to place a school-based health center in the school. Fortunate enough to secure the grant, Marian and company opened the center in the school with a staff of four: two nurse practitioners, a social worker, and a receptionist. Any student who completed and returned a one-page application signed by a parent or guardian was eligible for services.

The center met with immediate success. Within the first year of operation, two-thirds of the student body was receiving multiple medical services at the center. Tracking and collecting data on student absenteeism, Marian and her staff began to see a dramatic increase in student attendance rates. Without question, one important factor was the school-based health center. Students were now receiving immediate medical attention that wasn't available to them in the community.

When addressing the total child, the role of quality and timely medical care cannot be overstated. Meeting the physical and mental health needs of children contributes to academic advancements in the classroom. The earlier the health care intervention, the more dramatic the results.

Safety as a Top Priority

Steve, the principal of a large urban high school, ran into his old acquaintance, Brian. As they caught up on their children and careers, Steve learned that Brian was now a member of the board of education in his suburban community. Brian mentioned that he had heard about the school resource officers (SROs) who operated in Steve's school. "I'm glad we don't have the problems in our school district that you face in the urban environment," he exclaimed. "We don't need police; our schools are already safe."

After listening patiently as Brian went on about the conditions that necessitated a police presence in urban schools, Steve told Brian that he had missed the point. Although Steve's school did have police officers, their primary role was to build relationships with the students.

Relationships, which are the foundation of understanding, are more easily fostered between law enforcement and youth in the absence of a crisis, arrest, or investigation. The concept of SROs in schools is consistent with the *community policing* approach, in which police officers are assigned a particular neighborhood so they have the opportunity to develop relationships with its residents. These stronger police-community relationships in turn reduce the crime rate. SROs work the same way in schools: Over time, students and officers have opportunities to interact, develop positive relationships, and coexist peacefully, thus reducing the overall incidence of violence.

In many communities, children and adolescents have few—if any—positive interactions with the police. The Drug Awareness and Resistance Education (DARE) Program, a 6-week drug resistance program offered by local police departments to fifth-grade students, is perhaps the only positive experience young people have with police. Their next interaction may well be the result of a traffic violation or some other negative incident. Policy makers should do everything in their power to place an SRO in every school in this country—not simply for safety reasons, but rather for the purpose of developing positive relationships between law enforcement and children and youth.

As Steve shared his viewpoint, Brian began to look at the role of police officers in schools through a different lens. Although critics might argue that armed officers in the school create a prison-like atmosphere, the opposite is true. Officers trained to work in schools can build a foundation for greater understanding and community. In fact, research indicates that SROs who have had training in relationship skills are viewed as an asset to the school (James & Ciurczak, 2004; U.S. Department of Justice, n.d.).

Leveraging the System

Linda had been a principal of an inner-city school for 3 years. More and more students were coming to the school with previous involvement in the criminal justice system. Many of these students had been assigned a probation officer with whom they would meet regularly outside of school. Since the probation officers often had an overwhelming caseload, there was typically little follow-up with the school. Basically, Linda saw an overloaded system that could not prevent the students at her school from falling deeper into the criminal justice system.

Linda and her leadership team decided to try and leverage the system to better meet the needs of the students and ultimately reduce recidivism. The data they collected indicated that students were being seen by a number of different probation officers, both at the adult and juvenile levels. Linda met with the regional coordinator of probation, and they arranged to consolidate services so that students would be served under just one adult probation officer and one juvenile probation officer. By doing this, they were better able to coordinate services and meet the needs of these students.

However, Linda had another concern: many students were missing a full day of school to meet with their probation officers. Also, probation officers were often not getting a realistic picture of the students' lives at school because their information came only from the subjective reports of the students themselves. To address these issues, Linda and the leadership team created office space in the school's guidance department for the probation officers. These officers established certain days of the month to meet with students, and Linda arranged for her assistant principals to attend these meetings.

This new system ensured that accurate information about the students' academic and behavioral performance at school could be shared. It fostered positive relationships between school staff, probation officers, assistant principals, and youth offenders. As a result, students' needs were better served and student recidivism decreased.

Banker's Hours

Sebastian was a principal of a large suburban high school. One of his goals was to examine and implement creative ways to make the school-community connection a reality for students. He believed that helping students see the connection between what they do in school and the "real world" was essential. Students often say,

"Why do I need to learn this? I'm never going to use it." External stakeholders within the community can be part of the solution for building relevance into the curriculum.

With this in mind, Sebastian asked a local bank executive to serve on his school's curriculum support team, and the bank executive agreed. Together, they worked with a local savings and loan to open a branch office of the bank within the school. From the inception of the idea to the planning of the grand opening, the students were active and involved participants. Students worked collaboratively with teachers and representatives from the bank to determine its marketing strategy and ways to attract high school students as customers. The design of the space was a particular challenge and students worked side-by-side with the architect to ensure that the design was both functional and appealing. In addition, students were instrumental in designing the curriculum to ensure that it was relevant to real-world application. Working with the school's business education teachers, employees from the bank, and students, Sebastian and the curriculum support team were eventually able to turn total responsibility for all aspects of the branch office over to the students.

External stakeholders within the community can be part of the solution for building relevance into the curriculum.

The results of this project were overwhelming. Within a few months, almost half of the student body had opened accounts at the school's branch office. The officers from the savings and loan were extremely pleased—they had the opportunity to establish the possibility of long-term customers and simultaneously provide a valuable learning experience for youth within the community. The students also benefited by gaining valuable employment and career skills, as well as a greater appreciation for activities that took place in the classroom. In the redesigned curriculum, the classroom was run as if it was a business since the classroom was in fact an operating branch office of the bank. Students held different jobs and the bank rotated positions frequently to give students the opportunity to experience multiple roles.

A WIN-WIN SITUATION

Bringing the outside in clearly benefits all parties. By involving local businesses and other groups such as law enforcement, the school is able to access valuable community resources and create opportunities for students that otherwise may not have been available to them. In turn, students become more actively involved in both student and community life. And students who are involved and invested in their schools are more likely to succeed.

Next Steps: Collaboration

The old adage of *many hands make light work* is true if everyone is working together. We apply the adage to the process of developing and applying the best possible solutions to organizational problems by saying *many minds make better solutions*. Collaboration works when it is a basic assumption of the organizational culture, and people will do it naturally when the message is "No one person has all of the answers, not even the boss." Consider using PBL as a way to build leadership in your school while simultaneously addressing a problem.

1. The principal has inherited a small but tightly knit group of problem teachers. Out of a faculty of 40, these 8 teachers always sit together in the back of the room at every faculty meeting, never volunteer for anything, and make fun (behind the scenes) of those who participate. These teachers are mediocre, but not incompetent, and are tenured. They are popular with students because they are "fun" and their classes are less challenging. At faculty meetings, they undermine any serious discussion by turning it into a joke. They are all active in the teachers' union—one in a district leadership position. The principal's task is to engage these faculty members as meaningful contributors in improving the school. What advice would you give the principal?

2. Using your school (or a school with which you are familiar), rank order the list found on page 87, placing the area most in need of improvement or attention in your school at the top of the list. Then, for each of the top three areas chosen, list two ways in which you might involve community resources that would positively impact your student body.

3. At your next meeting, place a pressing issue on the agenda. Choose an issue that has received much attention but little action associated with identifying possible "solutions." Before the meeting begins, speak to one or two of the most vocal critics of the problems caused by the issue and ask if they would be interested in spearheading a task force assigned to finding some possible approaches to addressing it and bringing them back for discussion with the whole group. Then, as you address the related agenda item, praise your new task force leaders for their willingness to take an active role and also express your support for the work of the task force. Participate as much as you can with the task force—but let the leaders lead. Let them bring the task force findings before the body and go from there.

CHAPTER FIVE

PILLAR FIVE: ACCOUNTABILITY AND RESPONSIBILITY

Ultimately, we are all held to a standard.
—Steven Edwards

"You're picking on me!" As Sam walks down the halls of his high school accosting students who are chronically late to class, he hears this phrase uttered over and over by disgruntled students. His response is always the same: "Of course I'm picking on you. And I will continue to pick on you until you're able to consistently make it to class on time." Is Sam a callous principal with no sensitivity to students? No—the reality is just the opposite. It would be easier for Sam to sit at his desk. Instead, no matter how many times he sees the same faces in the hallways after the bell, Sam continues to hold them accountable. What better way to show students that he cares, and what better way to build strong relationships with them?

Like students, teachers and administrators need to be held responsible and accountable. Too often, the blame game is played out, with high schools pointing fingers at middle schools and middle schools in turn passing the blame on to elementary schools for sending them students who are unprepared to succeed academically. Educators at all levels point to parents, and politicians at all levels interject their various opinions about who is to blame for low student achievement.

In reality, the responsibility rests with each of us, and collectively we have the capacity to improve schools for all students. Establishing clear, measurable, and attainable goals and objectives that are developed by the collective efforts of all stakeholders creates the opportunity for achievable outcomes for which we can realistically hold ourselves accountable. This chapter describes the challenges school leaders face as they are held accountable to the four sets of stakeholders identified by Strike (2007): the legislature, parents, the professional community, and the school's community. After that discussion, the chapter ends with an example of a principal who decided that responsibility must be shared.

Strike's framework asserts that the school leader has a responsibility not only to fulfill legal mandates, but also to create institutions that respect the professional judgment of teachers and the voice of parents, both as individuals speaking for their own children and as a collective speaking for the school community. There is no escaping the reality that school leaders must—and do—serve more than one master.

Establishing clear, measurable, and attainable goals and objectives that are developed by the collective efforts of all stakeholders creates the opportunity for achievable outcomes for which we can realistically hold ourselves accountable.

THE LEGISLATURE

Alexander and Alexander (2005), in their seminal work *American Public School Law,* report the chronology of how state legislatures became the builders and financiers of the American public schools. The first stirrings were during the colonial period:

> Even though there was some governmental recognition of the benefits of education, as evidenced by a 1642 statute in Massachusetts in which all parents were charged with seeing to the education of their children, and later by a 1647 statute in which the legislature required certain towns to appoint a teacher and permitted taxes for education, by and large early colonial legislatures tended to ignore education....

> According to Horace Mann, it was at the Massachusetts Bay Colony in the seventeenth century that the concept of public universal education was born. Mann said that "it was reserved for 'the Fathers' to engraft that great principle in the laws of a country, as a maxim of government, *that all the people of a State should be educated by the State.*" (p. 22)

In the United States, state legislatures traditionally establish the laws that define the nature and place for schools as well as the human resources organizations that provide the services. State constitutions, however general or specific they may be, outline how schools are operated and maintained. The federal government, although interested in schooling from early on, has been inclined to give the states free reign over education. Recently, however, the federal government has stepped up and made a case for attaching more strings to federal dollars flowing into the states.

NCLB brought educational accountability and responsibility to a new level. The federal government established clear guidelines and consequences regarding academic measurement and performance. Around the country, the influence of NCLB is evident. From superintendents to classroom teachers, the way professional educators do business has changed, with the primary focus now on high-stakes testing, and the law's long-term implications yet to be determined.

Within the context of whatever state or federal mandates exist, however, continually working to meet the academic, social, and emotional needs of an ever-changing student population is always at the forefront of education. The responsibility for the successful education of our youth rests with each of us, and it will only be achieved through the collaborative efforts of all stakeholders. Although the challenge is great, the rewards are even greater.

THE PARENTS

Accountability is a two-way street. In successful schools, there is ample support from many sectors, including parents and community members. Sergiovanni (2009) maintains that successful schools enjoy a high level of *leadership density*—"the total leadership available from teachers, support staff, parents, and others on behalf of the school's work" (p. 179). Although those who lead and serve from within the school system are accountable to parents to operate schools so students will learn and become successful, parents must also be accountable to their children by taking a proactive role in supporting the school.

The principal remains the key player when it comes to establishing open lines of communication with parents. In every example described in this book, the school leader built a rapport with all stakeholders by maintaining an open-door policy. A school culture built on trusting relationships among all stakeholder groups creates a safe and student-focused environment. In such schools, parents are more likely to feel accountable to support their children, and they also expect accountability from administrators, teachers, and staff.

Glen and Sharon became principal and assistant principal of Central High School (CHS), a rural school serving 1,100 students. The previous leadership team had allowed school discipline to become lax; rules about leaving school property were not being enforced. Daily school attendance was at an all-time low of 75%, and many students would habitually come and go from the building without checking in or out.

In the first staff meeting, Glen raised the question of students leaving the building. Teachers' responses to the question surprised Glen; they expressed despondency and helplessness about school discipline in general. Glen could perceive their frustration at the lack of support from the previous administration.

Glen and Sharon discussed the problem and decided that they needed help from the parents. They hosted a spaghetti dinner for the community. Students waited tables, cafeteria staff prepared the meal, and all teachers were required to attend. After the crowd had gathered and eaten, Glen began to talk about the students of CHS and how important they were to him. During his talk, Glen wove in the importance of students getting to and staying at school. He said that he and his faculty and staff needed help with this situation. The response was overwhelming. One after another, parents rose in support of changing the current practice; several reported that they worried about their children walking around downtown during school hours.

Glen put together an attendance task force headed by Sharon and made up of parents, faculty, and staff. He charged the task force with reviewing current policy. After three meetings, the attendance task force reported back to Glen with recommendations. The most meaningful recommendation was to take roll at the beginning of every period of the day and report the data in real time.

The way students came and went from CHS changed dramatically. Glen's show of trust and request for collaboration had propelled faculty and parents to action on behalf of their students. This was a cultural change prompted by holding all stakeholder groups, including parents, accountable.

A school culture built on trusting relationships among all stakeholder groups creates a safe and student-focused environment.

Professional Standards and the Professional Community

The professional education community has been moving toward a standardized approach for almost all areas of education for some time. While most of these standards focus on students, many different organizations focus on setting standards for how we prepare teachers and administrators. The National Council for the Accreditation of Teacher Education (NCATE) is chief among them. NCATE has been the umbrella organization for accrediting teacher education programs since 1954.

The Educational Leadership Constituent Council (ELCC) is NCATE's Specialty Professional Association in educational leadership. ELCC is responsible for developing and using standards for evaluating educational leadership programs in NCATE-approved universities. There are currently four professional associations affiliated with ELCC: the National Association of Elementary School Principals (NAESP), the National Association of Secondary School Principals (NASSP), the American Association of School Administrators (AASA), and the Association for Supervision and Curriculum Development (ASCD). Since the mid-1990s, ELCC has developed two sets of standards to evaluate educational leadership programs; the most recent was last updated in 2007. All programs seeking national recognition by the ELCC are reviewed under these new standards.

No matter what you think of national standards for the preparation of educators, it is important to note that many professionals came together from all sides of education to discuss what standards are important and how to professionalize education across the board. The national standards for principal preparation programs that were developed serve to equalize rigor of programs and quality of emerging leaders. Too often, however, standards are developed only at the state and national levels, and the interpretation of them at the local level can vary significantly.

Understanding that these variances occur and wanting to prevent it from happening locally led one district to work with their state regional educational center to ensure that the state standards were both understood and applied with the fidelity and rigor with which they were intended. District office educators, principals, and representatives from the state regional education center worked collaboratively to design a rubric based on the state leadership standards. The rubric served as a tool to assist the district educators, principals, and state regional education center team assessing individual and collective leadership competencies. After the rubric was in place, the team collectively determined what they would accept as evidence and artifacts for each level of the rubric. The development of the rubric and the associated identification of evidence and artifacts became a powerful tool to improve leadership across the district and provide a platform for discussions of what effective leadership looks like.

Membership in professional organizations is generally optional at the institutional and personal level, but school leadership is not a job for the isolationist. Discussions among colleagues about how to be better leaders are an important characteristic of all professions.

The School's Community

Relationships with the larger community must also receive attention from the school. Bagin, Gallagher, and Moore (2008), in *The School and Community Relations,* wrote the following:

> In recent years the importance of school-community relations and overall school public relations has grown rapidly. As a number of states, starting with Minnesota in 1988, offered choices for parents in determining where to send students, more and more board members and school administrators recognized the importance of letting people know about the opportunities in their schools. The violence eruptions in schools have prompted more concerns to try to help people responsible for the schools communicate more effectively to help prevent disasters. (p. 1)

There is no better reason than student safety for school leaders to be accountable to the surrounding community. As we have said before, everyone in the community is a stakeholder of the public schools. Because school leaders work with and are accountable to community business owners, police, fire departments, social services, and juvenile courts, they are in a unique position to be the hub for the safety and well-being of the communities' young.

School leadership is not a job for the isolationist.

Alexa was the principal of a small (approximately 300 students) elementary school in a medium-size midwestern city. For years, the neighborhoods around the school had experienced high levels of crime and violence; although there was a police presence, it was often reactionary rather than proactive. Out of concern for her students, Alexa decided to organize key stakeholders in the community to address the incidents of crime and violence.

The school already had a Parent Teacher Association (PTA) that met each month, and Alexa thought this would be a good place to start. At the next PTA meeting, she placed the topic at the top of the agenda, but the parents initially seemed to be passive about Alexa's concern. However, Alexa had done her homework. She had collected data on incidents of crime and violence in the neighborhoods surrounding the school, and the data caught the parents' attention. Now the parents felt a sense of urgency to take action, but were unsure as to how to proceed. Alexa raised the question, "Who else has an interest in this issue?" The parents and teachers at the meeting brainstormed a list of the following interested or impacted parties:

- District office officials
- Police
- Elected officials
- Local businesses
- Faith community

With their list in place, they identified specific individuals from each of the groups and drafted a letter to be sent by Alexa on school letterhead to those individuals indicating their concerns and a few data points, and requesting that these individuals attend the next PTA meeting to form a community action team to address the challenge of crime and violence in the community. The selected individuals did attend the next meeting (after second and third phone calls by Alexa to those who did not respond to the initial letter), formed an action team, and worked collaboratively to develop an action plan with mutual accountability.

School administrators, teachers, staff, parents, and community members all have a vested interest in making their public school a place where students are safe and can and do learn. Given this dynamic, we are all responsible for and accountable to one another.

SHARING RESPONSIBILITY

Everyone in the organization contributes to the health of the organization, either positively or negatively. When individuals and groups play a role in addressing issues, solving problems, and generally contributing to the overall well-being of the organization, everyone benefits. If we want to create positive change, everyone must accept a level of responsibility and accountability. Consider the following example.

Becky was a seasoned building administrator who, as a common practice, encouraged her staff to come to her office with their concerns. It was rare when a staff member came alone. Usually the staff member would state his or her complaint in the presence of a supportive colleague, and then Becky would fix the problem, whatever it was.

It became evident to Becky, however, that more and more people were bringing their problems to her and expecting her to fix them. Becky realized that she had created a monster. She needed to shift a share of the accountability and responsibility to the staff members who expressed the concerns. She quickly had an opportunity to put her new approach into action.

Four second-grade teachers made an appointment to see Becky. They stated that they had concerns about students wandering the hallways after school. They had noticed that the numbers of students had increased, the noise level was getting higher, and the overall behavior of the students had deteriorated.

Becky told the teachers that she heard their concern and agreed that, without question, this situation needed to be addressed. She added she would personally visit their wing of the building the next day to assess the situation for herself. The teachers liked that; they felt it meant that Becky was taking responsibility for the situation. But they were unprepared for her next comment: She suggested setting up a task force to analyze the problem and recommend some solutions, and asked them (since they had an interest in the issue) to serve as the task force's core members. Furthermore, she appointed the lead spokesperson from the group as the chairperson. As the teachers left Becky's office, she reminded them that they were either part of the problem or part of the solution.

Word of Becky's actions quickly spread through the school. Her decision significantly reduced the number of staff coming to her office with problems. Other staff members respected the decision that Becky had made and, as the taskforce team met, they were successful in coming up with a solution to the hallway problem. With this success, teachers determined that they could take responsibility for addressing other challenges the school was facing.

New task forces were created by teachers and leadership began to be distributed throughout the school.

Becky's goal was not to reduce communication, but rather to have individuals share in responsibility and to be held accountable for playing a role in the overall effectiveness of running the school. Becky's actions had laid the foundation for that goal.

Next Steps: Accountability and Responsibility

Each of us has the responsibility to think on, speak on, and act on what should be done for the greater good, and we are all accountable to one another. This is a basic tenet of all of the major religions of the world. What flows from this idea is that a group of people immersed in a culture where the good of all comes before the good of one has more viability in a volatile world. Consider the following PBL exercises:

1. The new principal came to a high-performing school with a long history of excellence. The population of the school and its surrounding community was about 80% middle- or upper-income White families and 20% low-income African American families. The principal started the year by beginning the process of helping faculty articulate its belief statements. The first belief statement offered was "All children can learn." The principal was surprised when several of the lead teachers on the faculty would not embrace this statement. The teachers felt strongly that some special education and African American children were unable to learn—and it was "mean" to

expect the children to perform to high standards. What suggestions would you give to the principal to help those teachers and the entire faculty take personal and professional responsibility for the learning of *all* children?

2. Take a personal inventory of your own actions:

   (a) Do I hold high standards for myself and others in all matters of organizational work and behavior?

   (b) Do I look for better ways to do things—then test those ways and share what I learned from both my successes and my failures with others?

   (c) Do I truly seek to know and understand my colleagues at work and allow them to really know me?

   (d) Do I challenge myself to do things that will enhance my professional skills in areas where I could do a better job? Do I encourage others to help me identify such areas?

   (e) Do I hold myself and others responsible for sharing new ideas that could help the organization move forward?

CHAPTER SIX

PILLAR SIX:
CONSISTENCY AND
REDUNDANCY

Practice makes perfect.

The above saying is correct—*if* you correctly practice the skill you are trying to perfect. Too often, though, the skill is practiced incorrectly, and the intended outcome is never achieved. A better adaptation of this adage would be, *Practice makes permanent, so be sure to practice the right things.*

In *Life's Greatest Lessons: 20 Things that Matter,* Hal Urban wrote about replacing negative habits with more positive ones:

> Trying to break a bad habit through sheer willpower rarely works. What has proven to be far more effective is replacing the habit—substituting it with a behavior that's more

positive. This technique has been around for hundreds of years, at least as far back as Benjamin Franklin's time. In his famous autobiography, Franklin explains a technique he used for eliminating his worst habits and replacing them with good ones. He made a list of thirteen qualities he wanted to have. He put them in order of importance and wrote each one on a separate page in a small notebook. He concentrated on each quality for a week at a time. If he failed to practice that particular virtue satisfactorily, he would record little black marks next to it. By working steadily at each one, he eventually eliminated the need to make the marks. By this time he had acquired the virtue. By using this technique, Franklin's new habits replaced some of his old ones. (2003, pp. 51-52)

To practice the same skill or behavior over and over again will likely make it a permanent habit. The key is to practice the right behaviors—those that move us in the direction of expertise.

To achieve this level of expertise in any skill or behavior requires consistent reinforcement and repetition. Successful organizations exhibit consistent and redundant courses of action for positive organizational outcomes. They stay the course and are consistent in the delivery of their message, product, and/or service. This chapter gives several examples that illustrate the importance of consistency and redundancy in day-to-day operations and school improvement.

THE IMPORTANCE OF MAINTAINING ROUTINES

Human beings are creatures of habit. They need the comfort of a known structure to operate day in and day out. Consistency reduces stress and contributes to a sense of calm. Consider what happens when students have a substitute teacher. Climate is negatively affected because consistency has been interrupted.

When Marian arrived at her new principalship of a 1,500+ student high school, the district had a practice in place of providing a half-day staff development session once a month. Marian observed that the disruption of the daily routine caused by the monthly staff development day was causing problems.

On the professional development days, all seven classes were held, but each class was now 30 minutes rather than 45 minutes. In addition, passing time between classes was reduced from 5 to 4 minutes. This reduction may not sound like much, but Marian understood that it was a challenge for students to get from class to class in 4 minutes.

The result of the shorter classes and shorter passing times was a reduction in instruction and an increase in tardiness to class, which in turn affected instructional time. Furthermore, Marian observed that, on professional development days, teachers still taught seven periods and now were also required to participate in a 2-hour in-service session. They were tired, and little was gained from the staff development program. The schedule the students and staff were accustomed to had been altered and consistency had been broken; the results were detrimental to both students and staff.

When Marian discussed the issue with the staff, they agreed with her assessment. Marian recommended to the district professional development committee that the practice of using half-days be abolished and that an additional full-day professional development session be instituted. The end result was the addition of 3 full-day staff development days over the course of the school year. All parties were satisfied and benefited from the change.

By focusing on consistency and redundancy, we can increase student academic achievement and reduce disruptive behavior.

The teaching team structure common in middle schools and in the early years of some high schools is another recognition that consistency can improve academic achievement. In the early 1990s, educators realized that ninth-grade students were having an increasingly difficult time making the transition to high school. This was one of the motivating factors for the institution of 2-year interdisciplinary academic teaching teams. In some schools, incoming ninth-graders are placed on teams of approximately 100 students who stay together for 2 years with the same four subject-area teachers in English, mathematics, science, and social studies.

This contrasts with the typical high school routine that provides little consistency and redundancy. In a school with a seven-period day, a student typically has seven different teachers to report to, each with a different set of rules, teaching styles, and expectations. Imagine if a classroom teacher had seven different principals to report to, each one with a different set of expectations and management style. Or imagine if a principal had to report to seven different superintendents. The point is clear: the challenge would be difficult, to say the least.

Such a high degree of inconsistency sets students up for failure. In contrast, the teaming model allows students to spend 2 years with the same core group of teachers. The teachers also enjoy a high degree of consistency, with a common planning time to develop common policies and procedures for academics and behavioral requirements. Well-designed structures built with a common purpose provide consistency, safety, and support for those who operate within them.

CONSISTENCY FROM DAY ONE

By focusing on consistency and redundancy, we can increase student academic achievement and reduce disruptive behavior. However, this can't simply be the consistency of a "rule" posted in every classroom. Instead, what staff members *do* to encourage good behavior and in reaction to misbehavior is a critical element, since consistency between word and action strengthens the message.

If you start out with clear expectations and deliver a consistent message, you will more likely achieve your intended goals.

Marian, the principal referred to earlier in this chapter, received a telephone call about a week before the start of the school year. The call was from a newspaper reporter who was doing a story on the chronic problem of student attendance on the first few days of school. The reporter asked Marian what, if anything, her school would be doing differently on the first day to entice students to attend. He mentioned that he had already posed the same question to a number of Marian's peers, and some had stated that they had planned special events for the first day. In fact, one school planned to have a band playing on the school's front lawn and to serve a picnic-style breakfast for the students.

Marian agreed that attendance on the first day was important. Attendance every day was important, and Marian communicated this message to students by emphasizing that their high school program was not a correspondence course. Active participation and engagement can only occur when students are present in school.

However, Marian told the reporter that her school did not plan to engage in gimmicks to entice students to attend the first day. When school started at 7:30, the first and foremost task of her staff would be to engage students in academics as soon as they entered their classrooms. It was important to convey the message that academics were the priority the moment students walked into the building on the first day—as well as every day for the rest of the year.

Change is not a sprint, but rather a marathon; you must be in the race for the long haul.

As it turned out, the school that opened the year with a band and a picnic ended up having a mini-riot on that first day. When it was time to go into the building, the students decided that they would rather stay outside and continue the party. Eventually, the police were called in. It was memorable first day for that school, and the reporter had another story to write.

The saying "What you do in September, you live with in June" rings true. If you start out with clear expectations and deliver a consistent message, you will more likely achieve your intended goals. The key is to communicate the message from day one and then stay the course.

SUSTAINING CONTINUAL RENEWAL AND GROWTH

Consistency and redundancy are essential to establishing sustainability in school programs and improvement initiatives. Staying the course is the modus operandi that transforms an initiative from "new" to "the way things are done around here." Once you have decided on your desired outcomes and designed a plan on how to get there, achieving success largely depends on your ability to stick to the plan, even through the common phenomenon that Fullan (2004) calls implementation dip. In *Leading in a Culture of Change,* Fullan explains that, with any change initiative, there is a tendency to slip backward before you move forward. To move through that dip takes time and requires leadership to focus on consistency and redundancy.

Attempts to institutionalize change always meet resistance. One of the best ways to overcome resistance is to remain consistent in the delivery of the message. The more people who deliver the same message on a regular basis, the stronger the message will be and the sooner it will become part of the school culture.

Organizational change is not about a quick fix, but rather about creating long-term, sustainable change that transforms a school— or any organization, for that matter. Change is not a sprint, but rather a marathon; you must be in the race for the long haul. Successful schools do not plateau; they continue to move forward with steady, consistent improvement. They achieve this by clearly establishing expectations, empowering others, and committing to stay the course day in and day out.

Next Steps: Consistency and Redundancy

Behaviors do not become habits until we do them repetitively, and they become entrenched in our minds and become almost automatic responses to everyday activities. Unfortunately, consistently and redundantly doing things the wrong way also develops a natural response, although one built on bad practice. The goal is to identify a best practice and make it the habit. This is true for individuals and organizations. The sixth pillar ties together all of the previous five to give a picture of best practice that can become habitual on both the personal and organizational levels.

1. The new principal realizes that consistency is a major problem for the school. Every teacher is an island of isolation with his or her own method for counting tardiness, calling roll, grading, assigning homework, managing the classroom, dismissing class, preparing for a substitute, and supervising the halls and cafeteria. What suggestions would you give the new principal in establishing consistency and redundancy in these areas?

2. Rate yourself on a scale of 1-10 in each of the traits listed below, with 10 signifying the highest level of effectiveness and frequency you perform each, and list several examples of how you incorporate these traits into your routine responsibilities as a school leader:

(a) Understand the importance of trying to get better every day and communicate it to others.

(b) Never forget that all eyes are on you as a leader and try to always act accordingly. Do the right thing.

(c) Always support and encourage others and hold yourself and everyone else to the same standards.

(d) Practice, practice, practice.

CHAPTER SEVEN

BRINGING IT ALL TOGETHER

Don't wait for your ship to come in. Swim out after it.

Thus far, we have discussed a set of principles that we call the Six Pillars of Dynamic Schools:

- Communication and relationships
- Leadership and empowerment
- Planning and evaluation
- Collaboration
- Accountability and responsibility
- Consistency and redundancy

The pillars are based on our study of organizations, our teaching in this area, and our collective practical experiences. These core principles serve as the foundation of successful, sustainable organizational growth and improvement. Each of the Six Pillars can be addressed in isolation based on your specific needs, yet collectively they will contribute to accelerating change. There is a natural synergy that exists among the Six Pillars; used in combination, they complement each other.

Organizational change is not about a quick fix, but rather about creating long-term, sustainable change that transforms a school.

We are well aware that there are countless books written about how to improve organizations. As we travel around the United States and internationally, we have had the opportunity to spend too much time in airports. Airport bookstores draw us in, and each of these stores has a section of the latest books on how to improve organizations. These books typically focus their attention on two areas: organizational growth and leadership. These same areas are the key to improving schools and the basis of the Six Pillars.

However, two characteristics make the Six Pillars framework an especially strong model for school improvement in our rapidly changing world. First, the pillars evolved through reflection on the experiences of schools that needed to engage in dramatic change—and did so successfully. Second, as discussed earlier, an intersection can be drawn between each of the pillars and the four macro trends shaping modern life—Globalization, Localization, Digitalization, and Fragmentation—that provide the context within which our schools operate. Table 7.1 represents an effort to describe each of these intersections in ways that demonstrate how they impact the everyday life of schools. The table poses questions that link the Six Pillars with the macro trends and is part of a set of metrics that schools can use to assess their effectiveness in each of these areas. Individuals or schools that would like more information about this instrument may contact the authors.

Table 7.1. The Six Pillars and the Four Macro Trends

	Globalization	Localization	Digitalization	Fragmentation
Communication and Relationships	I feel uncomfortable when those I supervise know more about a particular topic than I do.	Those outside of our organization who work with us comment on our organizational culture.	Although I recognize the globalization of our world, most of my communication at work involves individuals who live in the same state/province as I do.	I have at least as much fun at work as I do in the other areas of my life.
	In a given week at work, I find myself saying out loud to others that I don't know the answer to something.	Our organization relies on the direct assistance of outsiders from around the world.	At work, I often re-examine ideas with which I previously disagreed.	At my primary work site, different rooms and offices all have the same "feel" to me.
	In a given week, I seek out someone for the answer to a question that challenges me.	Within our organization, we share with one another lessons learned from our problem solving efforts.	Our organization needs fresh perspectives on our work.	At my work, I experience feelings similar to those when I engage in personal recreation.
	I keep a list, whether on paper, in a computer, or inside my head, of individuals and their respective expertise upon which I rely.	Individuals who provide advisory assistance to our organization reflect diverse nationalities.		

Table 7.1. The Six Pillars and the Four Macro Trends (Continued)

	Globalization	Localization	Digitalization	Fragmentation
Leadership and Empowerment	I learn new technology skills from the experiences of others in my organization.	More than just a few individuals in my organization express feelings of being "left out of the loop."	Over the past year, I have established ties with international partners.	When making decisions at work, I rarely consider what our organization symbolizes.
	When someone in my organization has success with a new technology, we don't get around to celebrating it openly.	In my organization, I have to consider who doesn't get along with one another when forming new alliances.	Over the past year, I have suggested to those I supervise that they should establish ties with international partners.	In my organization, seemingly crazy ideas are considered at least briefly.
			When there is a failure in our organization, we simply move on rather than using up time to discuss it.	
			I celebrate publicly a subordinate's risk-taking even when it resulted in a failure.	

Table 7.1. The Six Pillars and the Four Macro Trends (Continued)

	Globalization	Localization	Digitalization	Fragmentation
Planning and Evaluation	In our organization, we have rejected popular technologies that fail to make our work easier and/or more enjoyable.	I know positive, personal anecdotes about most of my fellow employees.	Our strategic plan addresses ways of doing business that were not feasible without access to the World Wide Web.	In my organization, we are comfortable with our level of understanding of the cultures we serve.
		When employees from our organization have left to take a new job elsewhere, they infused some of our organization's values into the new one.	Somewhere in my organization, I can find records that summarize the lessons learned from a particular project or initiative.	
Collaboration	In my organization, when substantive, non-petty problems arise, no individual is blamed for it.	In our organization, the efforts of each individual who contributed significantly to the success of a project are recognized publicly.	I use the World Wide Web (e.g. Internet, email, etc.) to partner with individuals around the globe.	Our organization uses symbolic objects or events to recognize successes.

	Globalization	Localization	Digitalization	Fragmentation
Accountability and Responsibility	In our organization, we spend time testing with our stakeholders new ideas for technology use.	In our organization, we take the time to identify what a particular individual's strengths and needs are in order to best utilize him/her within the organization.	If a particular technology is working well in our organization, we should not mess with it.	In my organization, I have to learn the "hard way" what others' limitations are.
	In my organization, I do not feel any pressure to be innovative.		At work, I experiment with new technologies several times a year.	During meetings in our organization, individuals often will share that a particular subject matter is not "their strongest area of expertise."
Consistency and Redundancy	Most days, I am so busy doing good work that I forget work-related anxieties.	In my organization, my colleagues and I often share with one another technology-related skills and knowledge.	In my work, I'm too busy with important work to find time to complain about my job.	Even when I disagree strongly with a colleague's decision or action, I still treat them cordially.

Table 7.1. The Six Pillars and the Four Macro Trends (Continued)

HIGHLIGHTS OF THE PILLARS

The first pillar is *communication and relationships.* Relationships are the key to personalizing the school and improving its overall climate. Each day we have the opportunity to engage or disengage students, staff, and other stakeholders. Using effective communication skills and fostering relationships significantly contributes to any change initiative.

Leadership and empowerment constitute the second pillar. Someone once said that leadership is like beauty: it is hard to describe but you know it when you see it. For the purposes of this book, we have focused primarily on leadership as the ability to empower individuals in our schools. We discussed the fact that good leaders take responsibility for sharing reality with colleagues and other key stakeholders. They may be visionaries with their heads in the clouds, but their feet are firmly planted on the ground. Accepting and being able to articulate reality is clearly the hallmark of a successful leader.

Planning and evaluation is the third pillar. Effective planning will result in positive change; poor planning can be disastrous, resulting in lost time, money, and credibility. Evaluation is a critical component of planning; it provides the feedback necessary to make adjustments for continuous improvement.

Collaboration, the fourth pillar, is essential for long-term sustainable change. Fullan (2004) suggests that creating a collaborative culture builds trust, collegiality, and professionalism. Either we find ways to work together or we remain in the age-old trap of isolation that has plagued the education profession for years. Over the last 20 years, U.S. corporations and schools have experimented with numerous management techniques used in other countries that have collaboration as a focal point. The levels of success of these attempts vary; individualism is valued in American culture, and changing that paradigm takes time and energy. With that said, we believe that it is worth investing the time and energy to build a collaborative culture that will have all in the organization focused on continuous progress toward a common goal.

The way the education field views the fifth pillar, *accountability and responsibility,* has undergone significant change in the last decade. NCLB contributed to a higher level of accountability. With accountability comes responsibility, and responsibility sometimes scares people. Whatever changes are made to NCLB in the future, accountability will be part of the discussion. However, if we are truly responsible for and to one another, a better education system is our common goal.

Consistency and redundancy constitute the sixth pillar. Consistency means staying the course to achieve your vision. Many organizations have a tendency to jump from one initiative to the next. There is constant confusion, and members of the organization are never clear on the direction the organization is heading. Schools are not immune to this phenomenon. To move forward, we must clearly articulate a vision, identify initiatives that drive towards that vision, and then stick with those initiatives long enough to realize measurable outcomes.

It is important to understand that consistency does not mean that we do not make changes along the way—quite the contrary. Successful organizations adapt and adjust in response to changing conditions and remain open to new ideas and innovations, but they do not allow anything to deflect them from their vision and mission.

STAYING AHEAD OF THE CURVE

"So what. Now what."
—Dr. Ashby Kilgore, Superintendent of Newport News
Public Schools (VA)

It is at this point that many books on leadership and organizational change finish. A theoretical structure has been provided, often accompanied by practical examples. But such an approach focuses too little attention on the "So what. Now what." step so aptly highlighted by Dr. Kilgore. Where do you and your school go from here?

The Next Steps included at the end of each of the pillar chapters were intentionally included to get you started. Given thoughtful attention, they can help you and others in your school focus on areas that need improvement and also support capacity building. But, as with any organizational improvement effort, it's not simply how good the guidance is. Instead, you and your staff determine the "Now what." For some schools, the Six Pillars could provide the framework for a year-long reflection on elements critical to staff, other schools may choose to focus on one particular pillar that addresses a concern within the school.

Throughout life, we all have choices. A leader could sit back, wait, and see what happens, or he or she could have the vision to seize the moment and move forward. If we do the first, we are making the choice to become part of somebody else's plan. But if we choose to be proactive, we are the masters of our own fate.

Begin with the notion that all things can be improved. Regardless of where a school is today, we can decide to make it better.

Working on each of the Six Pillars of Dynamic Schools requires a level of risk-taking, as well as the self-discipline to stay the course in the face of adversity. But after all, that's what leadership is about: the willingness to step out of your comfort zone and face the challenges head on, to confront reality and design a plan to achieve collective goals. By studying the elements of each of the Pillars, you can lay the foundation to achieve both individual and collective goals.

There are many schools that consider themselves "good": They have met required proficiency on state testing, and they are free from any major behavioral issues. Thus, they are content to move along at this level. Other schools are not willing to accept being on a plateau, but challenge themselves to improve. What we're talking about is staying ahead of the curve—not accepting good as good enough, but rather constantly challenging ourselves to move forward. This can be achieved by applying the principles we have discussed in this book.

Given the sweeping political and economic changes occurring at the local, state, and national levels, conditions are right for visionary leaders to make a real difference. Using the Six Pillars of Dynamic Schools as a framework for envisioning a hopeful future is the first step for leaders who will be at the forefront in shaping a better world.

REFERENCES

Alexander, K., & Alexander, M. D. (2005). *American public school law* (6th ed.). Belmont, CA: Thomson West.

Augustine, N. (2008). Falling off the flat Earth? In *Thrive. The skills imperative* (p. 8). Washington, DC: Council on Competitiveness.

Bagin, D., Gallagher, D. R., & Moore, E. H. (2008). *The school and community relations* (9th ed.). New York: Pearson Education.

Bossidy, L., Charan, R., & Burck, C. (2002). *Execution: The discipline of getting things done*. New York: Crown.

Bracey, G. (2009). *Education hell: Rhetoric vs. reality.* Alexandria, VA: Educational Research Service.

Clemens, W. C. (2000, Summer). Alternative futures AD 2000-2025. *OECD Observer*. Retrieved from http://www.oecd.org/countrieslist/0,3351,en_33873108_33844430_1_1_1_1_1,00.html

Collins, J. (2001). *Good to great: Why some companies make the leap and others don't.* New York: Harper Collins.

The Connecticut Institute of Municipal Studies. (1998, June). *Exemplary practices in Connecticut schools.* Hartford, CT: Author.

Connors, R., Smith, T., & Hickman, C. (2004). *The Oz Principle: Getting results through individual and organizational accountability.* New York: Portfolio.

Covey, S. R. (1989). *The seven habits of highly effective people: Powerful lessons in personal change* . New York, NY: Simon & Schuster.

Friedman, T. (2006). *The world is flat: A brief history of the 21st century.* New York: Farrar, Straus, & Giroux.

Fullan, M. (2004). *Leading in a culture of change.* San Francisco, CA: Jossey-Bass.

Goodlad, J. I. (1976). *Facing the future: Issues in education and schooling.* New York: McGraw-Hill.

Goodlad, J. I. (1997). *In praise of education.* New York, NY: Teachers College Press.

Hilliard, A. (2002). Urban Education Conference in Washington, DC.

James, B., & Ciurczak, G. (2004). *Student voices* (Research Brief). New Paltz, NY: New York State Center for School Safety.

Kouzes, J. M., & Posner, B. (2006). *A leader's legacy.* San Francisco: Jossey-Bass.

Lewin, R., & Regine, B. (2000). *The soul at work.* New York: Simon & Schuster.

Monroe, L. (1997). *Nothing's impossible: Leadership lessons from inside and outside the classroom.* New York: Perseus.

The Pew Global Attitudes Project. (2006). *Truly a world wide web: Globe going digital* (2005 Pew Global Attitudes Study). Washington, DC: Author. Retrieved from http://pewglobal.org/reports/pdf/251.pdf

Phillips, T. D. (1992). *Lincoln on leadership: Executive strategies for tough times.* New York: Business Plus, Hachette Book Group.

Sergiovanni, T. J. (2009). *The principalship: A reflective practice perspective* (6th ed.). New York: Pearson Education.

Strike, K. A. (2007). *Ethical leadership in schools: Creating community in an environment of accountability.* Thousand Oaks, CA: Corwin.

Toffler, A. (1990). *Power shift: Knowledge, wealth, and violence at the edge of the 21st century.* New York: Bantam Doubleday Dell.

Urban, H. (2003). *Life's greatest lessons: 20 things that matter.* New York: Simon & Schuster.

U.S. Department of Justice. (n.d.). *Community policing topics.* Retrieved May 13, 2009, from http://www.cops.usdoj.gov/default.asp?Item=106

Wallis, C. (2006, December 18). How to bring our schools out of the 20th century. *Time.* Retrieved from http://www.time.com/time/magazine/article/0,9171,1568480,00.html

Zhao, Y. (2008, December 11). *Contextualizing global citizenship.* Keynote presentation at meeting of the Kentucky Leadership Academy, Louisville, KY.

ORDER FORM FOR RELATED RESOURCES

ERS

Quantity	Item Number	Title	Base Price	ERS Individual Subscriber Discount Price	ERS School District Subscriber Discount Price	Total Price
				Price per Item		
	0761	*Six Pillars of Dynamic Schools*	$30.00	$22.50	$15.00	
	0472	*The Informed Educator: High-Achieving Schools: What Do They Look Like?*	$9.60	$7.20	$4.80	
	0771	*Superintendent's Briefing Book, 2010*	$96.00	$72.00	$48	
		Shipping and Handling* (Add the greater of $4.50 or 10% of purchase price.)				
		Express Delivery* (Add $20 for second-business-day service.)				
*Please double for international orders.					TOTAL PRICE:	

SATISFACTION GUARANTEED! If you are not satisfied with an ERS resource, return it in its original condition within 30 days of receipt and we will give you a full refund.

Visit us online at www.ers.org for a complete listing of resources!

Method of payment:

☐ Check enclosed (payable to ERS)   ☐ P.O. enclosed (Purchase order #_____)

☐ MasterCard   ☐ VISA   ☐ American Express

Name on Card: _____   Credit Card #:_____

Expiration Date: _____   Signature: _____

Ship to: (please print or type)   ☐ Dr.   ☐ Mr.   ☐ Mrs.   ☐ Ms.

Name: _____   Position: _____

School District or Agency: _____   ERS Subscriber ID#: _____

Street Address: _____

City, State, Zip: _____

Telephone: _____   Fax: _____

Email: _____

Return completed order form to:
Educational Research Service • 1001 North Fairfax Street, Suite 500 • Alexandria, VA 22314-1587
Phone: 703-243-2100 • Toll Free Phone: 800-791-9308 • Fax: 703-243-1985 • Toll Free Fax: 800-791-9309
Email: ers@ers.org • Web site: www.ers.org

SUBSCRIPTIONS AT A GLANCE

SAVE TIME. SAVE MONEY. MAKE BETTER DECISIONS

www.ers.org

The ERS Advantage Annual Research Service enables you to. . .

- Enhance your effectiveness as decision makers
- Make research-based, data-driven decisions with confidence
- Learn about programs and practices that will improve student achievement

Simply choose the subscription option that best meets your needs:

✓ **ERS District Advantage**—an annual research and information service that provides education leaders with timely research on priority issues in preK-12 education. We do the work so that you don't have to! For one annual fee, you will receive ERS publications and periodicals, *ERS Custom Searches*, and 50% discounts on ERS resources. Also, we will send your ***entire*** staff the *ERS e-Bulletin* and *Informed Educator Series* to keep them up-to-date on current educational topics and important issues. Another benefit is 24/7 FREE access to the *ERS e-Knowledge Portal* that contains more than 1,600 educational research-based documents, as well as additional content uploaded throughout the year.

✓ **ERS Leaders Advantage**—an individual annual service designed primarily for school administrators, and school board members who want to receive a personal copy of new ERS studies, reports, and/or periodicals published, as well as 25% discounts on other resources purchased.

✓ **Other Education Agency Subscription**—available for state associations, libraries, departments of education, service centers, and other organizations needing access to quality research and information resources and services.

We Want to be Your Research Partner. Let ERS work for you!

Your ERS Subscription benefits begin as soon as your order is received and continue for 12 months. For more detailed subscription information and pricing, contact ERS toll free at **800-791-9308**, by email at ers@ers.org, or visit us online at www.ers.org!